ADRIFT

ADRIFT

A TRUE STORY OF LOVE, LOSS, AND SURVIVAL AT SEA

Tami Oldham Ashcraft

with Susea McGearhart

DEY ST.
An Imprint of WILLIAM MORROW

HarperCollins books may be purchased for educational, business, or sales promotional use. For information, please email the Special Markets Department at SPsales@harpercollins.com.

Originally published as *Red Sky in Mourning* in 2002 by Hyperion.

FIRST EDITION

Library of Congress Cataloging-in-Publication Data has been applied for.

ISBN 978-0-06-286820-6

18 19 20 21 22   LSC   10 9 8 7 6 5 4 3 2 1

To the memory of my grandfather Wally J. Oldham,
the solid foundation in my life,

and to Richard Sharp . . .
who will live in my heart forever.

ONE

On the Firing Line

Hearing the clank of the anchor shank as it hit the bow roller, I turned my attention to Richard. With a grand gesture, he waved to me—"Let's go!" I shifted the engine into forward. As I nudged the throttle, *Hazana* gathered speed and we headed out of Papeete Harbor on the island of Tahiti. It was September 22, 1983, at 1330. In a month we'd be back in San Diego, California. If only I were more excited. I hated to leave the South Pacific. It wasn't that I didn't want to see my family and friends, it was just too soon. We'd only been gone from California for six months and had originally planned to cruise the South Pacific islands and New Zealand before visiting home again. This change in plan left me feeling ambivalent. But as Richard pointed out, this yacht-delivery job was a dream come true—too good to pass up.

Shouts from the shore drew my attention. Turning around, I saw some of our friends waving good-bye. I stood up on the helm seat and waved with both arms high in the air as I steered with my bare left foot. I felt a pinch on my big toe as Richard took the helm with one arm and put the other around my waist. I looked down into his China blue eyes. They were full of joy. He squeezed me close and kissed my pareu-covered stomach. I couldn't help but smile, he was like a young boy in his excitement.

"Anchors aweigh, love."

"Yep, anchors aweigh!" I chimed back.

My eyes teared as I gave one final wave to the friends on the wharf who now appeared as lampposts on the quay. The familiar knot in my throat was a reminder of how hard it always is to leave, the thought that you may never meet again. Even though we will be back soon, I reminded myself, our friends will probably not be there. Sailors don't stay long in one place—they travel on.

I took the wheel as Richard hoisted the mainsail. Taking a deep breath I scanned the horizon. The island of Moorea stood out to the northwest. Oh, how I loved the sea! I steered the boat into the wind, and the mainsail cracked and flogged as Richard launched the canvas up the sail track. With the boat turned downwind, the roller-furling jib escaped as slickly as a raindrop on glass. *Hazana* comfortably heeled over. What a yacht this Trintella is, I thought. Forty-four feet of precision. So plush compared to our *Mayaluga*.

Watching Richard trim *Hazana*'s sails, I reflected on how hard it had been for him to say good-bye to *Mayaluga*. He had built her in South Africa and he named her after the

Swazi word meaning "one who goes over the horizon." She had been his home for many years, and he had sailed the thirty-six-foot ferro-cement cutter halfway around the world. *Mayaluga*'s lines were sleek and pleasing to the eye, her interior a craftsman's dream, with laminated mahogany deck beams, gleaming from layers of velvety varnish, and a sole—floor—made of teak and holly.

To avoid thinking too much about what we would be leaving behind, we had both kept busy during our last days aboard *Mayaluga*. I was preoccupied with packing all the clothes and personal things we would need in the two hemispheres we'd be sailing through and visiting in during the next four months: T-shirts for fall in San Diego. Jackets for Christmas in England. Sweatshirts for early winter back in San Diego. Pareus and shorts for our return in late January to Tahiti. Richard had focused on preparing *Mayaluga* for the months ahead without us.

She'd be safe in Mataiea Bay. Our friend Haipade, who lives at the bay with his wife, Antoinette, and their three children, promised to run her engine for us once a week. We took special care to prop up all the cushions and boards so the humid air of Tahiti could circulate. We left the big awning up to help protect her brightwork from the intense sun and cracked open a hatch under the awning.

When we left *Mayaluga* my back was turned to her as Richard rowed us to shore. I could not see his eyes through his sunglasses, but I knew they were misty. "I know Haipade will take good care of her," I assured him.

"Yeah, he will. This bay is completely protected."

"Besides, we'll be back in no time. Right-o?"

"Right-o." He smiled at me for having mimicked his British accent.

Now, aboard the *Hazana,* the wind shifted and I altered our course 10 degrees. Richard leaned down in front of me, blocking my view. "You okay?"

"Sure."

Going behind me, he uncleated the halyard to raise the mizzen sail. "Isn't this great?"

It was great. Great weather, great wind, and great company. His optimism was contagious. Isn't this what sailing's all about? I thought. Adventure. Going for it. Hell—time would fly.

The log entry for our first day out read: "Perfect day. Tetiaroa abeam. Full moon. Making 5 kts. in calm sea under all plain sail."

Day Two, we were making six knots under the mainsail and double headsails. Later in the day we had to sheet all the sails in hard to combat the north-northeast wind.

Day Three, we were still pounding into the wind. *Hazana* held up well, but we felt fatigued. A thirty-five-knot squall hit later in the day. We rolled in the genny, dropped the mainsail, and sailed under staysail and mizzen.

The clap of a wave against *Hazana's* port bow startled me. I ducked my head to block the spray. There was no way we'd

Richard and me aboard *Mayaluga*

be easing the sheets—spilling the wind from the sails to make the ride more comfortable—for we had committed to deliver *Hazana,* and it was San Diego or bust.

I watched the aqua and teal ocean colors commingle and dissolve into the deeper seas' midnight blue. San Diego or bust, I mused. I always return to San Diego—home sweet home. It seemed so long ago that I had worked in the health food store and graduated from Pt. Loma High. I remembered how I grabbed that diploma and split—cut every cord keeping me grounded. All I wanted to do was cross the border into Mexico and surf its fantastic waves. Back then, it was Mexico or bust. I smiled, remembering how important it was for me to be free, on my own. I bought a 1969 VW bus,

Yacht *Hazana*, a Trintella 44'

named her *Buela*, and talked my friend Michelle into taking off with me. We threw our surfboards on the roof rack and breezed through customs for Todos Santos with its promise of great waves to surf and adventures to be had. That was fall 1978.

Michelle and I made camp on the beach at Todos Santos with other American surfers. For a month, all we did was surf, eat, party, and sleep. But, when Michelle couldn't shake the obligations she had waiting for her back home any longer, she reluctantly left, hitching a ride north.

I made friends with a local family, the Jimenezes. I learned enough Spanish to get by and had fun teaching their five kids English. They lived and farmed on leased land. I'd help them pick tomatoes and cilantro, and in exchange, they'd allow me to keep the overripe tomatoes to make salsa to sell to the gringos on the beach. My little business was lucrative enough to subsist on, so I didn't have to dip into my savings.

With so many Americans coming and going I never felt lonely and I never felt scared just being alone. Every week or so I would drive into Cabo San Lucas or La Paz for supplies. In Cabo there was a little sidewalk greasy spoon that served up a great Mexican breakfast. Lots of the gringos off cruising boats hung out there. The restaurant was a funky cinder-block building with a take-out window on the side. All of the seating was outside. There was a menu near the window and next to that was a huge bulletin board the size of a sheet of plywood. All kinds of messages and announcements were pinned onto this board.

One morning I saw an ad that caught my attention. "Crew wanted. Sailing experience not necessary. Cooking a must. Departing for French Polynesia at the end of the month." I didn't even know where French Polynesia was, but the sound of it lured me. "Contact Fred S/V *Tangaroa*."

"Hey," I yelled to Drew, a cruiser I'd met, "what does S-slash-V mean?"

"S-slash-V? It means sailing vessel, babe."

"Thanks, babe."

Ah, so the *Tangaroa* was a sailing vessel. Not having a VHF radio to hail *Tangaroa,* I walked to the beach and studied the many sailboats at anchor. As they swung with the current I could read their names, and soon I spotted *Tangaroa.* Its dinghy was tied to the stern, so I knew its owner was still on board. I kicked back on the warm sand and waited for someone to row ashore. After some time had passed, I saw an older man get into the dinghy and row in.

After he had secured the skiff on the beach, I approached him.

"Are you Fred?"

"Yes," he said, quickly looking me over.

"I saw your want ad for crew and I'm interested."

He invited me to have a cold cerveza up at the Muy Hambre cabana. Over the cerveza I told Fred the only boat I had ever sailed was my dad's Hobie Cat in San Diego Bay, so I didn't know a thing about sailing, let alone sailing across the ocean to a foreign port. Fred told me his boat was a custom-built Dreadnought 32. We discussed what my responsibilities would be on board, namely cooking and taking watches. I said that if what he really wanted was a "partner" I wasn't interested. He told me he was recovering from a Tabasco-laden divorce and the last thing in the world he wanted or needed right then was a partner. All I would need to do was cook and stand watch.

With all the cards on the table, we agreed to go on a shakedown cruise—a trip to see how I took to sailing. We sailed to La Paz, 170 miles away.

It was a fabulous, two-day trip. Fred was the gentleman he promised to be and I took to sailing like a fish to water. I signed on the *Tangaroa*. My mom was more apprehensive about my sailing off into the wild blue yonder than my dad, but she knew she couldn't stop me, just like she hadn't been able to stop me from coming to Mexico nine months earlier.

When I returned to Todos Santos, the Jimenezes said it would be okay for me to leave my bus parked there. Years later I learned it had become a livestock feeder. They'd dump food into the sunroof and open the side doors so it could spill out, conveniently feeding the pigs.

Fred and I left Cabo in March 1979. The passage down to the Marquesas was a wonderful learning experience for me. I spent a lot of time at the wheel learning the feel of maneuvering a vessel through the dense sea. The only bummer was that Fred and I were like oil and water. He, in his mid-fifties, liked classical music. I, nineteen, liked rock 'n' roll. He liked gourmet cuisine, I liked vegetarian meals. He was disciplined. I was carefree. He was an impressive man—posture perfect, body perfect, tan perfect. But all that was way too perfect for me.

One day, the horizon gave birth to volcanic peaks. I was breathless, seeing land after being surrounded for thirty-two days by nothing but blue seas and blue sky. Dense peaks split what had been a monotonous horizon line. It was a mystical sight that brought tears to my eyes. I wondered if this was how Christopher Columbus felt when he first saw land. Fred and I were barely speaking to each other by this time. I could hardly wait to get off *Tangaroa,* although I knew my desire to sail and explore had just begun.

Fred had told me we'd need to post an $850 bond upon checking into customs at Nuku Hiva, one of the Marquesan Islands of French Polynesia. But, being a novice traveler, I never dreamed my money, which was in pesos, was something the Marquesans wouldn't recognize as a trading currency. Fred posted the bond for me, but it meant I had to keep crewing and cooking for him. I mailed all my pesos to my mom in San Diego, who said via telephone that she'd convert them to American dollars and mail the exchange back to me in care of General Delivery, Papeete, Tahiti.

During that time, I met Darla and Joey, who were also crewing on a yacht. We became fast friends. A small group of us crewmates, all about the same age, ended up fraternizing, and to keep us from committing mutiny, our captains decided to buddy-boat together through the Marquesan Island group.

Fred and I were the first boat in our group to leave the

Marquesas and head for the Tuamotu Archipelago. It would be a three-day trip, and we deliberately timed it to arrive on a full moon, which would give us the most available light at night to navigate the atolls in case we arrived later than planned. Atolls are low-lying, ring-shaped coral reefs enclosing a lagoon. Because atolls are not easily seen and are surrounded by underwater coral reefs, they are dangerous to the mariner. Going aground on one can ravage the underside of a hull and sink a boat in minutes. The highest points on an atoll are the forty-foot palm trees swaying in the tradewinds. Due to the curvature of the earth and the fact that you are in a boat rolling with the sea, forty feet is not as obvious as a four-story building. Palm trees are the first indication to a mariner that solid ground is near.

It had been suggested that Fred and I look for certain ships and boats that had gone aground on these atolls, and to use the old hulks as points of navigation. Sailing past the wrecks on the reefs made me realize how important it is that everyone on board a boat be aware of the dangers and know how to navigate through hazardous areas. This was something I thought Fred knew.

Our first port of call was to be Manihi. Fred calculated it would be early morning before we spotted the atoll, giving us plenty of time and good light to find the lagoon entrance. When late morning came and we still hadn't seen anything, I started to get worried. It wasn't until one o'clock in the afternoon—when we saw the tips of palm trees blowing in the distance—that I could finally sigh in relief. Before long we were close enough to try to locate the entrance shown on the chart. We looked for a lull in the streams of white water, but all we saw was one long breaker. Fred explained that often waves break on either side of a lagoon's channel, making it hard to distinguish the cut in the coral polyps.

Fred and I took turns looking through the binoculars, voraciously scanning the breakers along the shoreline. Finally I climbed up the mast steps to the spreaders—the crossbars on the mast—and wrapped my legs and one arm around the mast, surveying the tropical isle through the binoculars. The land appeared continuous, with no cut. We sailed completely around the atoll and still did not find an entrance. My nerves were taut and Fred refused to admit we were lost. The sun was quickly setting.

Through heated words we both conceded that we must have been set—that is, pushed—to the west, and that we had circumnavigated the atoll Ahe instead of Manihi. So we agreed to sail on through the night to Rangiroa.

Both of us were on edge that night. We stayed awake, watching and listening for any waves that might be breaking across a reef. It was that night, in my fear, that I realized I never wanted to be in such a position again. I needed to learn to navigate.

At first light we saw our destination. It was like the palms were waving a special hello to me. Around midmorning, we located the pass. This time it was easy to see where the white water petered out and then churned up again. The shift in color along the shoreline made the channel obvious. We could see a yacht flying an American flag tied to the village loading dock. We maneuvered into the dock, with help from the couple off the other boat. I jumped onto the dock and exhaustedly said to the woman: "Man, am I glad to be here in Rangiroa."

"Rangiroa? You're not in Rangiroa. You're in Apataki!"

I was shocked. I leaped back on *Tangaroa* and went below to look at the chart. We had been set over a hundred miles southeast. What we had thought was the atoll of Ahe had actually been the atoll Takapoto, one of the atolls with no entrance.

I had now lost all confidence in Fred. I endured the five-day passage to Tahiti seething with anger toward him. My bags were packed two days before we arrived. I was eager to jump ship and leave the *Tangaroa* far behind me.

In Tahiti, I saw my friend Joey at an outside café; he told me he had signed on the schooner *Sofia* as a cook. I asked about *Sofia*. She wasn't a luxury liner by any means, he said, having been built in 1921, but she was awesome: a 123-foot, three-masted topsail schooner that was cooperatively owned. He added that the accommodations were rugged: The head, for example, was a toilet seat mounted on a metal bowl located on the aft deck, rigged to dump overboard. The galley had four kerosene burners and one large diesel stove, and the sink pumped only saltwater. Fresh water was allowed for drinking and cooking only, not to be wasted on such frivolous things as rinsing saltwater off the dishes.

The membership fee to join the sailing cooperative was

three thousand dollars. The cooks had to pay only fifteen hundred dollars. Joey set the hook when he told me the crew of *Sofia* was looking for someone to fill the other part-time cook's position. The next day I went to the schooner, applied, and got the position, becoming a permanent crewmember.

Though primitive, *Sofia* did have character. She carried a crew of ten to sixteen people. Her ribs creaked of history and adventure. She was heading for New Zealand via all the South Pacific island groups. Those days on *Sofia* were some of the best imaginable. The freedom of being on crystal blue water while sailing a square-rigger in glorious sunshine was magic. The camaraderie of the crew was well balanced. I was able to learn my sailing and boson skills and the basics of navigation, as well as cooking and how to help organize and instruct people on the art of sailing. It was like being in one of Southern California's greatest colleges: *Sofia*—U.S. "Sea."

Once in New Zealand we headed for a little town called Nelson, located on the northern tip of the South Island in Cook Strait.

While our *Sofia* was set to stay in Nelson for more than a year for repair work, I was offered a fishing job on a boat named *Pandora*. She was owned and operated by a former *Sofia* crewmember who stopped by the ship looking for crew. I signed on for an albacore season and ended up fishing two albacore seasons and a grouper season. The money was good, and I loved the challenging life of fishing—the sea popping like popcorn, with fish on every line.

While I was fishing, *Sofia* received a movie offer and the producer wanted the ship in Auckland for the filming. I had left most of my things—photos, letters, and clothes—on board, as I planned to reunite with *Sofia* in Auckland when the albacore season was over.

Sofia never made it. She sank in a bad storm off the northernmost tip of the North Island of New Zealand—Cape Reinga. One woman drowned when the ship went down. The sixteen survivors were at sea in two life rafts for five days. They were finally rescued by a passing Russian freighter, which located them thanks to their last flare.

I was at sea fishing when notified of the sinking. The boat I was on took me back to shore, and I flew to meet the *Sofia* crew in Wellington. All my plans had just sunk, along with an innocent young woman and a beautiful ship, with the snap of a finger. I wasn't sure what to do next. My visa, along with other *Sofia* crewmembers', had expired. I had nothing left but the clothes I had taken fishing and a few odds and ends. Even then my roots reached back to San Diego—only way back then, I had been out of the country for three years, not a mere six months, like now.

Richard poked his head out from below and said, "ETA thirty days, love."

I smiled broadly, for after having looked back on my inauspicious beginnings as a professional sailor, I was comforted by the faith I felt in Richard. Richard made it worthwhile being anywhere, even in the midst of this churning sea.

On the fifth day out of Tahiti, *Hazana* plowed the seas under genny and mizzen, making six knots. A deck fitting came loose and saltwater leaked onto the single-side band radio, shorting it out. The constant rolling from the northeast winds robbed us of our sleep. Our bodies were tense from deck gear clattering, the sails snapping and the rough ride.

The next day brought a reprieve. The wind came around to our beam and pushed us easterly, which is exactly what we needed. Richard wrote "Bliss" in the logbook. We decided to ease the sails and run off a little.

Basking in the sun, I twirled the lover's knot ring Richard had made me. Looking across the cockpit, I let my eyes wander over his muscular body. I admired his topaz-colored hair, wavy like the sea, and his short-cropped, full beard, bleached gold from the sun.

Richard wrote in *Hazana*'s logbook the next day: "I have now given up any illusions that the SE trades will ever do better than E! Now under 2nd reefed main, staysail, rolled up genny ($^1/_2$) & mizzen—flying 6 kts."

The Brooks & Gatehouse wind indicator gave out on Day Eight.

"I hope no more of this bloody equipment breaks down," Richard exclaimed to me.

"Could it be corrosion, or . . . ?"

"Sod corrosion. It's bloody high-tech electronics. The sun may not shine every day, but when it does, at least it will tell you exactly where you are."

"Then sod bloody high-tech electronics!" I teased, slapping my palm on the seat locker.

For the next three days *Hazana* flew. The full sails reflected the salmon-colored sun, and we enjoyed reading and relaxing, and getting some much-needed sleep.

Sunday, October 2, Day Eleven on *Hazana*, was special for Richard and me. At dusk, phosphorescence sparkled in the turquoise sea. We opened a bottle of wine and toasted our crossing the equator that day and entering the northern hemisphere.

Ahead of us shot a geyser of silver and translucent green spray: A large pod of pilot whales was coming to play with *Hazana*. We connected the self-steering vane and went to the bow to watch them leap and sing their high-pitched greeting. Grasping the stainless steel pulpit, Richard leaned against my back, his bearded cheek next to mine as the whales created beautiful crisscrossing streamers of chartreuse in front of us.

"Aren't the whales magical, love?" he asked, fascinated.

"Look how they surface and dive," he said as he slowly started undulating against my backside. As *Hazana* rose over the next swell, he whispered in my ear, "Surface . . ." And as the bow plunged into the trough, he said, "Dive."

"You could be a whale, Richard," I teased.

"I am a whale, love. See, I'm surfacing"—he nudged me forward, the rhythm of the whales sparking something amorous in him—"and now I'm going to dive."

As *Hazana* glided down into the trough, Richard reached around and untied my pareu as he clung onto me with his knees. He knotted the material onto the pulpit with a ring knot and cupped my breasts with his warm hands. I let go of the bow pulpit and stretched my arms out wide, *Hazana*'s fair figurehead.

"Ummm," I hummed.

"I want to dive with you, Tami," Richard murmured in my ear. "I want to surface and dive as these wild mammals do." I reached back and undid his shorts. They fell onto the teak deck.

With growing momentum we surfaced and dived, surfaced and dived, wild and free like the whales, before God, and heaven, and sky. *Hazana,* the queen whale, set the rolling rhythm we matched.

I later wrote in the logbook: "Bliss!"

Day Twelve: We hoisted the multipurpose sail, the MPS, which is very lightweight, and made four knots with the southeast trades finally catching us. The trades stayed with us for a number of days, pushing us to the east. We often saw whales, and now dolphins were showing their cheerful faces.

Dawn of October 8 broke gray, rainy, and miserable. The winds were unpredictable. They gusted from southeast to southwest and back around from the north. We were up near the bow checking the rig when a small land bird crashed onto the foredeck. The poor thing panted, unsteady on its short toothpick legs. Richard got a towel and dropped it over the bird. Scooping it up, he brought the bird to the cockpit, out of the rain and wind. Behind the windscreen, on top of the roof of the cabin, it squatted low, ruffling its wet feathers to warm its tired body. I crumbled a piece of bread, but the bird appeared too afraid to eat. The absurd winds must have blown the tiny bird far offshore. Richard later scribbled, "Cyclonic?" in the logbook.

As I read the word "Cyclonic?" in his log entry, I wondered what that meant to him. Could it be that we were sailing through some rogue whirlwinds? Is that possible? Had the little bird gotten trapped in the clocking wind without the strength or wherewithal to break free? Did Richard fear our getting trapped too? I'd been in plenty of clocking winds in the past few years and never considered them cyclonic. Richard didn't appear overly concerned, so I took it in stride too.

The next day the weather channel WWV informed us the storm they had been tracking off the coast of Central America was now being classified as Tropical Depression Sonia. They said it was centered at 13° N by 136° W and traveling west at seven knots. That put her over a hundred miles west of us.

WWV also warned of a different tropical storm brewing off the coast of Central America. They were referring to it as Raymond. In comparing our course, 11° N and 129° W heading north-northeast, to the course Raymond was traveling, 12° N and 107° W and heading west at twelve knots, Richard wrote, "Watch this one."

"Watch this one?" Storms come and go, I thought, often

petering out. I had learned that while fishing in New Zealand. Making note of it was Richard's way of staying on top of things. Unfazed, I just kept up with the odds and ends of our daily routine like cooking, cleaning, steering, and reading. It was especially joyful to sit in the cockpit writing a letter or two to friends left in Tahiti that I would later post in San Diego.

Near midnight the wind dropped. Then it came around to the east-northeast, which fueled Raymond's fury. We got hit with squalls and rain.

Monday, October 10, the wind veered to the north. At five in the morning, we changed our heading to north-northwest to gain speed. Our goal was to get as far north of Raymond's track as possible.

The wind died down to one to two knots, and we ended up motoring for four hours. But by noon, when the wind started screaming, we shut down the engine and put two reefs in the main. It was the smallest we could make the sail without taking it down, and we needed all the speed we could get. We had the staysail up and the genny was reefed also. We were plowing away at five knots to the north-northwest. Tropical Storm Raymond was now at 12° N and 111° W, heading due west. The bird was gone; it had flown the coop.

We decided to fly more sail in an attempt to run north of the oncoming storm. Taut lines, also known as jack lines, ran along each side of the boat from the bow to the stern. This gave us something to clip our safety harness tethers onto while working on the deck. We pushed *Hazana* to her max. There was no choice—we had to get out of the path of the storm. This storm was quickly surpassing the two horrendous storms I had experienced in the Pacific before I met Richard. I knew Richard had had his ass kicked while crossing the Gulf of Tehuantepec in Mexico on his way to San Diego. But this storm was rapidly turning into the worst conditions we had ever experienced together.

Richard and I got busy clearing the decks, just in case the conditions continued to worsen; we didn't need heavy objects flying around. We hauled the extra five-gallon jury-jugs of diesel down below and secured them in the head. They were heavy and it was difficult to move them in the rough seas.

At 0200 the next morning, the genny blew out. The ripped material thrashed violently in the wind; its staccato cracks and snaps were deafening. Turning on the engine and engaging the autopilot, Richard and I cautiously worked our way up to the mainmast, clipping our safety harness tethers onto the jack line as we went forward. "You slack the . . ."

"WHAT?" I yelled over the wailing wind.

"YOU SLACK THE HALYARD WHEN I GET UP THERE, AND I'LL PULL HER DOWN."

"OKAY," I shouted back, loosening the line.

Richard fought his way to the bow. I was terrified watching him slither forward. Gallons of cold water exploded over the bow on top of him, drenching me too. *Hazana* reared over the rising swells. The ruined sail whipped violently and dangerously in the wind.

Richard couldn't get the sail down. Finally he came back to me.

"She won't budge. Cleat off the end of the halyard, and come up and help me pull her down."

I did as he said and slowly worked myself forward on all fours, ducking my head with each dousing of saltwater. We tugged and pulled on the sail as it volleyed madly in the wind. Finally, after my fingers were blistered from trying to grip the wet sailcloth, the sail came down with a thud, half burying us. We gathered it up quickly and sloppily lashed it down. We then slid the number-one jib into the foil, and I tied the sheet—the line—onto the sail's clew. I made my way back to the cockpit making sure the line was not tangled—fouled—on anything.

Richard went to the mainmast, wrapped the halyard around the winch, and raised as much of the sail as he could by hand. I crawled up to the mainmast and pulled in the excess line while he cranked on the winch, raising the sail the rest of the way. It flogged furiously, like laundry left on a line in a sudden summer squall. We were afraid this sail would rip too. Once the sail was almost completely hoisted, I slithered as fast as I could back to the cockpit while Richard secured the halyard. I cranked like hell on the winch to bring the sail in. Richard came back to the cockpit and gave me a hand getting the sail trimmed. This sail change took us almost two hours. Richard and I were spent and wet, and we needed to eat. In between a set of swells, I slid open the hatch and quickly went down into the cabin before cold ocean spray could follow me in.

It was hot inside *Hazana* with all the hatches shut. She was moving like a raft in rapids. What would be simple to prepare, I questioned myself, instant chicken soup? As I set the pot of water on the propane stove to boil, I secured the pot clamps to hold it. I peeled off my dripping foul weather gear and sat down exhausted on the quarter berth.

Seven hours later, after the horrendous sail change, Raymond was still traveling west at latitude 12° N. Richard scribbled in the logbook: "We're OK." Obviously our northerly heading was taking us away from Raymond's westerly path, so we seemed to be getting out of harm's way.

All through the rest of the day, the wind and the size of the swells steadily increased. White water blew off the crests of the waves, creating a constant shower of saltwater spray. The ocean appeared powdered, as if white feathers had burst out of a down pillow. Tropical Storm Raymond was now being classified as Hurricane Raymond. That meant the wind was a minimum of 75 miles an hour.

At 0930 October 11, the present forecast put Hurricane Raymond at 12° N and spinning along a west-northwest course. Richard screamed at the radio, "WHY THE BLOODY HELL ARE YOU TACKING TO THE NORTH? STAY THE HELL AWAY

FROM US!" He had let down his stiff upper lip, and more than anger exploded—it was fear, raw bloody fear. My ribs constricted—an instinct to protect my heart and soul. Richard hurriedly recorded: "We're on the firing line." We flew every sail to its maximum capacity. I silently lamented over the useless torn genny; it was a sail we could have really used now because it was larger than the number-one jib. Richard told me to alter course to the southwest. If we couldn't situate ourselves above Raymond, maybe within the next twenty-four hours we could sneak to the south of the center and reach the navigable semicircle—the safer quadrant that would push us out of the spinning vortex instead of sucking us in. There weren't many options; we had to do something. It would be pointless to start the engine, for by now we were sailing way beyond hull speed as it was. Richard's nervousness and fear were obvious. I had never seen him like this. He mumbled a lot to himself, and when I asked what he said, he'd shake his head and say, "Nothing love, nothing."

But how could I ignore the way he scanned the sea to our east and repeatedly adjusted the sails, desperate to gain even a smidgen of a knot away from the forging Raymond? Adrenaline surged through me—fight or flight. There was no way to fly out of this mess, so it was fight. Fight, fight, fight.

At three o'clock that afternoon the updated weather report told us Raymond had altered its direction from west-northwest to due west with gusts to 140 knots. The afternoon sun sight gave us a second line of position. This indicated we would collide with Raymond if we continued on our southwest heading. We immediately came about and headed northeast again, trying to get as far away from Raymond as possible. The conditions were already rough enough. But to get clobbered by a hurricane would mean that we could lose the rig and really be disabled out here in the middle of nowhere. We did not fear for our lives, as we knew Trintellas were built to withstand the strongest of sea conditions, but the fact that one of us could get seriously hurt loomed unexpressed in both of our minds. With a shaky hand Richard inscribed, "All we can do is pray."

Later that night, the spinnaker pole's top fitting broke loose from the mainmast and the pole came crashing down, trailing sideways in the water. Richard and I scrambled to the mainmast trying to save the spinnaker pole. He grabbed it before the force of the water could break the bottom fitting and suck the pole overboard. It took both of us to lash all of its fifteen feet down on the deck. Creeping back to the cockpit we saw that a portion of the mizzen sail had escaped from its slides and was now whipping frantically in the wind.

"Jesus Christ, what's next?" Richard roared. He stepped out of the cockpit, clipped his safety harness onto the mizzenmast, and released the mizzen halyard. Once the mizzen was down, he lashed it onto the mizzen boom.

As he came back to me at the wheel, I noticed how dark the shadows were under his eyes. He tried not to sound sarcastic as he said, "Not much else can go wrong."

"We'll be okay. We'll be okay, love," I said, trying to convince both of us.

In the darkness, the ocean was highlighted with thick white caps of foam—a boiling cauldron. The barometer had dropped way down the scale as the wind's wail steadily increased, the seas becoming even steeper, angrier, more aggressive. We were terrified Raymond was catching us, but there wasn't a damn thing we could do about it but sail and motor as fast and as hard as possible.

We stayed on watch, taking turns going below to get whatever rest we could. Our muscles ached from fighting the wheel while trying to negotiate the pounding, erratic seas. Night had never lasted so long.

The next morning broke cinder gray with spotty sunlight shedding an overcast hue on brothy seas. Ocean spray slapped us constantly in the face. Wind was a steady forty knots. We reefed all sails and galloped with a handkerchief of a jib and mainsail. At least it helped steady the boat.

About 1000 the seas arched into skyscrapers, looming over our boat. The anemometer—the wind speed gauge—now read a steady sixty knots and we were forced to take down all sails and maintain our position under bare poles with the engine running. By noon the wind was a sustained one hundred knots. The churning spray was ceaseless. Richard came topside and handed me the EPIRB (emergency position-indicating radio device), as he took the wheel. "Here, I want you to put this on."

"What about you?"

"Tami, if we had two I'd put one on. Just make me feel better, and put the bloody thing on."

So, I did. I fastened my safety harness tether to the binnacle and steered while Richard went below to try to figure out our location now and get an updated position of the hurricane. All he could hear between the pounding and screech of the wind was static. There was no way he could risk bringing the radio outside with the sea constantly cascading over the boat.

Richard came topside, fastened his safety harness, and took the wheel. I sat huddled against the cockpit coaming, holding on with all my strength to the cleat where my tether was fastened. We were helpless while staring at the raging scene around us. The sound of the screaming wind was unnerving. The hull raised to dizzying heights and dove into chasms. Could the seas swallow us? The ascent of the boat over the monstrous waves sent the hull airborne into a free fall that smashed down with a shudder. I was horrified *Hazana* would split wide open. Finally I shouted to Richard, "Is this it? Can it get any worse?"

"No. Hang on, love; be my brave girl. Someday we'll tell our grandchildren how we survived Hurricane Raymond."

"If we survive," I hollered back.

"We will. Go below and try to rest."

"What happens if we roll over? I don't want to leave you alone."

"The boat would right itself. Look, I'm secure," he said, giving a sharp tug on his tether. "I'd come right back up with it."

I looked at his tether secured to the cleat on the cockpit coaming.

"Go below," he urged. "Keep your eye on the barometer. Let me know the minute it starts rising."

Reluctantly I got up, leaned out, and squeezed the back of Richard's hand. The wind sounded like jet engines being thrown in reverse. I looked at the anemometer and gasped when I read 140 knots. With my mouth agape, I looked at Richard and followed his eyes up the mainmast in time to see the anemometer's transducer fly into outer space.

"Hold on," he yelled and cranked the wheel. I tumbled sideways as the hull was knocked down. I fell against the cockpit coaming. An avalanche of white water hit us. The boat ominously shuddered from bow to stern.

Richard anxiously glanced at me, water dripping down his face, fear jumping out of his intense blue eyes. Behind him rose sheer cliffs of white water, the tops blown into cyclones of spray by the ferocious wind. My eyes questioned his—I couldn't hide my terror. He faltered, and then winked at me, thrusting his chin up, a signal for me to go below. His forced grin and lingering eye contact disappeared as I slammed the hatch shut.

I clung to the grab rail of the companionway ladder as I made my way down to the cabin below. The frenzied cadence of *Hazana's* motion prevented me from doing anything but collapsing into the sea hammock rigged to the table, and I automatically secured the tether of my safety harness around the table's post. I looked up at the ship's clock: It was 1300 hours. My eyes dropped to the barometer: It was terrifyingly low—below the twenty-eight-inch mark. Dread engulfed me. I hugged the musty blanket to my chest as I was flung side to side in the hammock. No sooner had I closed my eyes when all motion stopped. Something felt very wrong, it became too quiet—this trough too deep.

"OHMIGOD!" I heard Richard scream.

My eyes popped open.

WHOMP!

I covered my head as I sailed into oblivion.

TWO

1300 to 1600 Hours

WAAA-AH, WAAA-AH.

"Debbie, will you ease up on that sander, you're gonna burn it out."

"Tami, it's not cutting through."

"Well, change the sandpaper, Miss Lazy Bones."

"Lazy! This is hard work—besides, I'm starving."

"Okay, let's break for lunch."

The day was warm, as most summer days are in San Diego. The yard noise had quieted down for lunch, which gave the boatyard a peacefulness worth savoring. I dusted off the cockpit seat lockers with a rag and Deb and I sat down under the awning in the tepid shade. The sea breeze was light, tickling our hot, tanned skin. I pulled a tuna sandwich out of my lunch bag and a bright Red Delicious apple.

"Is that tuna again?" Debbie asked.

"Yes, white albacore. It's full of protein. You should try it sometime. Is that peanut butter again?"

"Yeah, full of protein too. *You* should try it sometime." Debbie took the largest bite humanly possible then chewed with her mouth open to irritate me. Suddenly, she almost choked. "Speaking of protein, check out this guy coming," she mumbled.

I turned and saw a honey blond lion walking up the dock. I liked his stride and how his strong, square shoulders moved with a purpose. He had on shorts and a T-shirt, and Topsider shoes with no socks. Glints of gold sparkled from the curly sun-bleached hair on his strong long legs. As he got closer, I noticed that his full trimmed beard was amber, like a patch of wheat. It was complimentary—attractive, how it framed his face. Liking how he looked, I quickly said to Debbie, "Don't say anything, okay?"

"Man, you're so paranoid. What am I gonna say—hey, good lookin'?"

"Just don't . . ."

Debbie and I were old friends and I knew it would be a miracle if she could keep her big mouth shut. But he started it, so she was off the hook.

"Lookin' good, ladies." His British accent surprised me.

"Thanks," Debbie smiled wide, and then coquettishly added, "Brightwork by Tami. Every job looks good. I'm Debbie and this is Tami. We're for hire."

"Right-o, Debbie." He smiled coyly. "I'll keep that in mind, that you two brighten up a boat in more ways than one."

"That we do, it's only one of our many talents. Huh, Tami?"

I felt myself blush as red as my apple and muttered, "Yeah, right Deb."

I could tell he was aware of my embarrassment by the way he cocked his head and smiled at me. "Other talents? That sounds intriguing."

I couldn't take the tête-à-tête any longer. Debbie always starts something. He probably thought we were a couple of boat bunnies. I could just choke her. Not knowing how to tactfully change the subject, I blurted out, "We have to get back to work."

"Hey . . ." Debbie started to protest, looking at her watch.

"We have a deadline to meet," I mumbled, stuffing the rest of my sandwich in the brown paper bag.

"Well, I don't want to hang you ladies up. It's been a real pleasure, one I hope to repeat when you're not so busy. Ta, Debbie. Ta, Tami."

I turned, looked at him, and was confronted with a great big smile. My heart leaped. His pale, baby blue eyes mesmerized me.

"Hey matie, what's your name?" Debbie broke the spell.

"Richard. Richard Sharp at your service. You can catch me at *Gypsy* on D dock."

"Well ta yourself, Richard from D dock." Debbie laughed.

He smiled warmly at her and said to me, "See you later?" I glowed red again and smiled like a fourteen-year-old before I could force myself to turn away. His footsteps echoed down the long wooden dock.

"Did you see the way he looked at you?" Debbie chirped. "He's in love."

"Oh, give me a break. You embarrassed the hell out of me saying, 'one of our many talents'! We're professionals, not dock babes. I'm so mortified, I could just fire you."

"Oh, not that again." Debbie sighed, throwing her sandwich's plastic bag into the five-gallon bucket we used for trash. "That was not a decent lunch break, I deserve overtime for today." She always had to get the last word in.

All that afternoon I thought about Richard. I was dating a couple of guys but they were just acquaintances. He must be talented to have been hired on *Gypsy*. I thought of his British accent, it was so exotic. I couldn't stop seeing his image in the reflection of the stainless steel winches as I varnished around them. I knew I wanted to see him again, but I hadn't developed the skill of trolling—reeling in guys like Debbie and some of my other friends had. Meeting him caused me to feel so good, so alive. I hoped I would see him again soon. I wondered what tool I could borrow from D dock.

I went home that afternoon with a feeling of euphoria. As I walked through the front door, the phone was ringing. "Tami, it's Bridget, boy do I have a gig for you."

"You do, Bridge-deck? Great," I said into the phone. "Where to this time?" I knew it was work, Bridget always thought of me first if she couldn't take a boat-delivery job. But this time my enthusiasm waned, for the image of Richard flashed through my mind and I knew if I accepted the delivery I wouldn't be seeing him for quite a while.

"This delivery sounds like fun," Bridget said. "It's a state-of-the-art racing sloop bound for the Big Boat Series at the St. Francis Yacht Club in San Francisco. Wish I could take it."

"Well, thanks for thinking of me again."

"The skipper is a South African named Eric. He's tall, dark, and handsome, but cool—no hanky-panky, unless, of course, you start it."

"Not me, not on the job."

"Smart girl. He'd like to meet you at seven thirty tomorrow morning at the Red Sails Inn restaurant to discuss the details. Can you make it?"

"Absolutely, Bridge-deck, thanks for the lead."

"Us first mates gotta stick together. Later."

When I walked into the restaurant I spotted Eric by the description Bridget had given me over the phone. Eric was sitting with two other guys whose backs were to me. I walked up and introduced myself. They had been there for a while and had almost finished eating.

Eric introduced me to Dan, the American, and then Richard, the Brit.

I thought I'd keel over. Blood rushed to my cheeks. Oh, not this revealing blush again, I thought. But there was nothing I could do to stop it. Richard smiled knowingly and halfway stood up while I took a seat across from him. Being this close to him, out of the bright sun, I noticed his eyes were not exactly baby blue, but darker—lapis lazuli. I had to look away, for if I stared any longer

I'd swoon. He was definitely affecting me in a way no man ever had before.

Eric asked me about my sailing history. "I've sailed from California, all through the South Pacific to New Zealand," I answered.

As Richard took a last bite of his omelet, I noticed his hands were rough, callused. He ate the European way, the fork upside down in his left hand, the knife in his right hand. He was older than I thought—thirties. What a doll.

The delivery crew would be Eric, Dan, and me, if I decided to take the job. I was disappointed to learn Richard wouldn't be going. He had a work deadline to meet on *Gypsy*.

As we talked about the delivery, my green eyes would wander to Richard's blue ones and discover them looking back at me. As the conversation wound down, in walked a petite, blond woman of about thirty. She came up behind Richard and put her hand on his back. I was crushed. I could tell he was attracted to me, but he was obviously taken. What was he doing flirting with me? Damn, I hated to be led on.

Her name was Lizzie, and she had a British accent too. She had come to deliver a message to Richard about work. I watched as Richard and Lizzie left together, and hoped my disappointment didn't show. Eric, Dan, and I made plans for the departure of the delivery cruise, which would be in five days.

Delivering the boat was a piece of cake. Even rounding notorious Point Conception, the water was flat calm. I was rather discouraged, because I had been eager to sail this hot-shot racing sloop, having never sailed with hydraulics before, let alone a stowaway mainsail. Dan and Eric were charming: Dan's sense of humor kept us laughing, and Eric's deadpan demeanor and boating skills kept us on track.

The elite St. Francis Yacht Club was right on the bay in downtown San Francisco. The location was spectacular, but the ambiance was unwelcoming—I felt out of it. The club was overrun by beauties wearing the latest fashion in boating attire. Through overheard conversations and a few conversations of my own, it didn't take long to figure out I had clocked more blue water nautical miles than seventy-five percent of the sailors there. I mused over the amount of money people would spend on trinkets like diamond rings, earrings, and pendants. The fancy gold-braided replicas of nautical symbols must have cost a fortune. Rolexes were on practically every wrist. It's a wonder the mirror in the ladies room didn't break from all the jealous glaring going on. It was obvious the competition wasn't just on the water. It didn't take me long to realize these sled-type racing yachts and the accompanying lifestyle weren't for me.

During the entire week of the delivery, I hadn't been able to get Richard off my mind. I subtly asked Dan questions about Richard and learned that he was thirty-four years old and that his relationship with Lizzie was on the rocks. Dan told me Richard had built his sailboat in South Africa and was circumnavigating the world when he decided to make a brief stop in San Diego to do a few repairs and earn a few bucks. This information piqued my interest again.

After cruising the South Pacific I had learned I had an artist's touch for varnishing. When I returned home from New Zealand and found there was a demand for yacht refinishers, I created a brightwork business. With the delivery over, Dan and I flew home. He was between jobs, so I hired him to help Deb and me in my thriving business. About a week after we returned from the delivery, Richard came by the job and asked Dan and me to join him for lunch; Deb was off that day. I stashed my brown bag and said sure, as casually as possible. I felt his eyes on me as I climbed down the ladder. He reached out and took my elbow as I stepped off the bottom rung. What a gentleman. My heart was caught—hook, line, and sinker.

One afternoon Richard came by the boat I was varnishing and asked me to have dinner with him that night. I hesitated and then told him I would be uncomfortable spending time with him while he was with Lizzie. He said he was asking me to dinner so we could talk and that he'd explain his relationship with her. Also, we could talk about the South Pacific. He would be sailing there next year, without her, and he'd love to pick my brain about it in a peaceful setting—like a quiet restaurant. I thought about saying no, but after all, I did know a lot about the South Pacific. And how could I say no, when my heart was sending a Morse code "Y-E-S?" I agreed to have dinner with him later that night.

I could hardly wait. The whole day I dreamed about Richard, his attractive good looks and buff body. I decided to wear my new peach-colored dress. It was simple, but I knew the spaghetti straps showed off my sculpted shoulders and arms—features I was proud of.

That evening over dinner, Richard explained to me that he and Lizzie had split up, but that she was still living on his boat while she made plans to return to England. He said that after meeting me he'd finally had enough of keeping his life and feelings on hold. After I had accepted his dinner invitation, he told her about it. She didn't like it, he confessed, but he explained to her he was ready to get on with his life and she should get on with hers. He apologized for her showing up and hoped it hadn't embarrassed me. The electricity between us, I'm sure, could be felt throughout the restaurant.

I felt much better, actually greatly relieved, that he would soon not be entangled with anyone. We had a wonderful evening and learned a lot about each other. He was an only child, with a half-sister, Susie, thirteen years older than he. I told him about my family and that I had been an only child until I was twenty-two, when my father had a son, Dane. But, more important, we learned of each other's great passion for the sea.

Richard had been born in England, in 1949, to an upper-middle-class family. His father was a retired navy man who did well after the war. His mother, unfortunately, had committed suicide when he was seven. His father soon remarried, and Richard thought of his stepmother as his "mum."

He was enrolled in a naval academy near London, being prepped as an officer in the navy. But once of age, he started to rebel against his father's wishes and the officers' demands and got kicked out for insubordination. He finished his schooling in another private school, but felt his father had never forgiven him for going against his wishes.

After Richard graduated he went to work for Olivetti, a manufacturing and sales company for electronic office equipment. He was good at sales and ended up buying a flat in London. He gathered a fine wardrobe and went through a few racy cars (and a few racy women too, I'm sure). But with a faraway look in his eyes, he admitted he had still felt unfulfilled. When a position in the company opened up in South Africa, Richard grabbed it. He adjusted quickly to South Africa and began to thrive on its beauty and diversity. But he despised apartheid and the way it limited people.

While with Olivetti, Richard met a man at a boatyard that built ferro-cement boats. They became fast friends, and soon Richard was offered a partnership in the yard. He eagerly took the job, quitting Olivetti with no regret. He loved being involved in building the thirty- to fifty-foot yachts. It was at this point that Richard met Eric, the skipper who had hired me to help deliver the racing sailboat to San Francisco.

I asked when Lizzie had come into the picture. Richard said he had met her in the Caribbean while he was waiting out the hurricane season. They hit it off, and Lizzie had decided to sail to San Diego with him. He had chosen San Diego after receiving a letter from Eric telling him what a great place it was to "winter over." Richard also was told he could prepare his boat for the South Pacific there and, with his skills, could easily find work on boats.

If Richard could have read my mind just then, he would have heard me thinking, *You came here because you were meant to find me.*

Richard totally captured my attention when his electric blue eyes penetrated mine, and he confessed Lizzie just wasn't the one—they weren't cut from the same cloth. He was born to see the world, and nothing—nobody—would stop him. It was clear he wanted me to know this right from the start.

I wondered what his plans would be after he'd sailed around the world. Would he just keep going around and around? I found a subtle way of asking this, and he said he didn't know for sure, but thought he would like to have a family one day. Maybe he'd even buy a little boatyard he'd seen in the south of England, if it went up for sale. But first, the South Pacific. He asked somewhat cavalierly whether I would like to go with him.

I laughed, but deep down inside, I tingled. *Was he serious?* "It's late; we need to slow down," I said, even though one part of me wanted to jump on his boat and leave for the South Pacific that night.

When we walked to my car, he leaned over and gave me a light kiss good night. It was like heaven, but hell too. I was dying to abandon all "good girl" protocol and throw my arms around him and never let him go. But, to my dismay, the sensible side of me won out, as it usually does. Lizzie needed to be out of his life before I could let myself in.

As I drove home I was smiling from ear to ear. I had never felt this way about any man before. I knew then and there I was going back to the South Pacific. "Mauruuru, mauruuru, mauruuru roa, atua. Thank you, thank you, thank you very much, God."

About a week later, Richard told me his grandmother had passed away in England, and he needed to go home for the funeral. Lizzie would be on the same flight. I felt he was trying to tell me it was over between us. Clenching my fists, I politely offered my condolences, turned around, and walked away. He caught up to me and explained Lizzie was going home to England and not returning to America, but he would be back soon. As Richard said good-bye to me, he said, "Tami, now that I've found you, I'll never let you go."

THREE

Coming To

I opened my eyes and saw blue sky and wispy, white clouds. My head throbbed. I went to touch it, but things, I didn't know what, lay on top of me, smothering me, crushing me. What was going on? I couldn't think, I couldn't remember. Where was I? My hammock hung cockeyed. I dangled near the floor. A can of WD-40 clanged against the table post. I moved, and a book splashed into the water.

I struggled to free myself. Dead weight pinned me down. Cans of food, books, pillows, clothes, a door, and panels of the main salon's overhead liner spilled off me as I struggled to sit up. I recoiled for I was covered in blood. I could feel a horrendous cut burning my left shin.

Where was I? What had happened? I was confused. I couldn't orient myself. The clock on the wall ticked a beat. 4 P.M.? That didn't seem right . . . My tether, still clipped onto the table post, confined me. I was obviously on a boat—what boat? My weakened hands frantically tried to unclip the tether.

Once unclipped, I strained to see around me. My vision was blurry; the pain in my head excruciating. Putting hand to brow, I flinched. I looked at my hand and saw crimson. Uncontrollable shivers engulfed me.

Laboriously, I crawled out of the labyrinth of wreckage. I stood up unsteadily. My back was wet and the water was over knee high. I felt faint. Slowly, one careful step at a time, I waded, negotiating my way through the obstacles floating in the two feet of water that lapped above the floor frames. This was crazy. The interior of the boat was chaotic. My God, what had happened? Books, charts, pillows, silverware, floorboards, cups, clothing, cans of food, spare parts, beans, flour, oatmeal—everything was either floating or stuck to the overhead, or to the bulkheads, or to the hull. The oven had been ripped from the starboard side of the boat and was now wedged into the nav station's bookshelf on the port side. What boat is this? Where am I?

I headed for the forward cabin—the V-berth. "Hello?" I called out. My voice sounded strange. I gaped at the turmoil in every nook and cranny. Cautiously moving toward the bow, I peeked in the head. There, in the mirror, I saw a frazzled image, its face covered in blood, the forehead cut wide open. Long strands of hair, wild and matted with blood, shot out from its skull. In fear, my hands flew to my mouth. I screamed. Then I screamed again. The ungodly sight was me.

"No!" I shouted, crashing into the bulkhead as I tried to escape.

I stumbled into the V-berth. Everything there too was topsy-turvy. The storage hammocks that hung on each side of the berth were overturned; spilled clothes lay every which way. Paperback books were off their shelves. The long mattress for the bunk was kinked, out of its place. Cans of food and even broken dishes lay strewn about.

I shook my head and wondered how the food and dishes got into the V-berth. In disbelief I backed into the main salon.

"Ray?" I apprehensively called.

Ray? I wondered where that had come from. It's not Ray. Ray's the hurricane. Hurricane? Hurricane Ray—Raymond. Where's Richard? Richard . . . "Oh my God . . ." But that's what he had said. . . .

Fear dropped me to my knees. I retched. Bilge water splashed against my cheek. Richard had not come below with me.

"Richard?" I screamed. "Richaaarrrd!"

I pulled myself to my feet, but had barely taken a step when the heel of my foul-weather boot slid. I fell against the salon table and threw up again. I looked at the ship's clock once more and desperately tried to concentrate on its second hand jumping: one thousand one, one thousand two. It read 1600 hours—4 p.m. Wait, that's not right! my rattled mind screamed. It had been one—one in the afternoon. "My God. . . . Oh, Richard . . . Richaaarrrd?" I wailed as I crawled toward the companionway ladder, my hands splashing water in every direction as I knocked food, cushions, books, whatever, out of my way.

"RICHARD? RICHARD?" I screamed over and over, choking on my words.

The companionway ladder had broken off its latches—it lay sideways against the nav station seat. I pushed it to the floor, out of my way, and climbed up on the back of the settee, screaming Richard's name. The companionway's main hatch was torn from its sliding tracks, leaving a gaping hole. As I hoisted myself up into the cockpit, I hit my head on the boom, which was blocking the entryway. "GODDAMN IT!" I howled and then painfully climbed over it.

There I saw Richard's safety line secured to the cleat on the cockpit coaming. The tether hung over the side of the hull. My God, could he be on the other end?

I lunged for the safety line, grabbed it tight, and yanked hard. It flew into the cockpit, the metal making a sharp *craaack* against the fiberglass. There lay the bitter end—the D-ring had parted.

Desperately I looked in every direction. Where was the howling wind? Where was the pelting rain? Where had it all gone? The ocean swell was a slow rolling six-feet, not monstrous like it had been.

I became a lunatic. Forcing the seat lockers open, I threw cushions, anything that would float, overboard. He's out there somewhere. Maybe he's alive. Oh God, please . . .

"Take this. And this. And this . . . HOLD ON RICHARD, I'LL FIND YOU."

I clambered below and grabbed more cushions, pushing them up through the main entry. Crawling back topside, I heaved it all overboard. The debris undulated in the otherwise empty sea. Adrenaline raced through my body, causing my heart to pound furiously.

Spotting the man-overboard pole attached to the mangled stern rail, I raced to it and struggled desperately to get it untied. I threw the pole as far out into the sea as I could. I was so weak. The orange flag bobbed in the swells.

He could be alive; it's only been three hours.

His last plea, "Ohmigod," roared in my brain. It must have been a huge wave. Larger than those forty-five-foot monsters. A rogue wave. We rolled, and Richard . . . Oh, my love . . . God, you wouldn't—you couldn't . . .

"RICHARD? RICHARD, WHERE ARE YOU?" I surveyed the ocean all around me, to the edge of the hazy horizon. Nothing encroached on the battleship gray sea—the troughs were empty, shallow bowls. "PLEASE, PLEASE, PLEASE." He was nowhere to be seen.

Hazana was ravaged. The mainmast was gone except for a four-foot piece still attached to the main boom. The tabernacle, a metal housing used to raise and lower the mainmast, lay on its side, a huge five-foot piece of torn deck attached to it. The large two-inch clevis pin that had been holding the foot of the mast in the tabernacle lay on the deck, sheared in half. "Oh my God," I wailed as I looked down through the gaping hole into the main cabin, seeing the hammock I had been lying in and all the floating debris. The mizzen mast was in the water, banging against the hull, held on by the starboard—right side—shroud. Stainless steel rigging hung overboard, with the roller-furling jib and staysail trailing in the water. A couple of stainless steel one-inch stanchions were tweaked like soda-pop cans. The rest were snapped in half like toothpicks. The lid to the in-deck propane locker was missing, and the propane tanks were gone.

"My God . . . Richard? Richard?" I howled.

I looked all around. " 'Richard? Richard?' "

Oh please, God, please. My legs gave way—I hung onto the boom and retched again.

He couldn't be gone. The dry heaves choked me. In total fear I clung to the boom and lay dazed, my cheek against the cold aluminum.

Get up. Move. An inner voice slammed into my thoughts.

Bawling, I crept over the broken-down boom, reached into the companionway, and groped for the binoculars. Miraculously, they were still strapped in their place.

After slithering back over the boom, I stood bracing myself, thinking, "I can save him, I can save him," as I scanned the ocean around me with the binocks. I could not stop trembling: The eye holes of the magnifying glasses pressed hard against my skull, drumming against my eyebrows.

I peered in every direction. All I saw was a vast desolate sea, with rolling six-foot swells. Nothing, not one goddamned thing, was out there.

Try the engine! the inner voice barked.

I pulled out the choke, adjusted the throttle, and pushed

the engine's start button. Nothing. Not even a grunt or grind. I didn't realize how much hope I was holding that the engine would start. My nerves spasmed and my stomach convulsed. When I hugged myself I felt the EPIRB still attached to my waist. I fumbled to unbuckle it. I couldn't center my mind. How does this thing work?

Remove the guard. Press the switch. Nothing. I stood up and held the radio device in the air. Nothing. I turned it in circles. Nothing. I sat down and started over.

With jittery hands I put the guard back on and then took it off. I pressed the switch and held the EPIRB up. Fumbling, I pulled out the batteries. With trembling fingers I wiped off the connectors and then put everything back together. Nothing. Damn it!

Water. The EPIRB needs water. Yanking open the seat locker I could see the bucket lying deep in the hole. It was the bucket Richard and I had used to pour saltwater over each other to cool off. Stretching, I grabbed the line on the bucket.

Holding the stern rail I threw the bucket into the water, scooped up as much saltwater as I could lift and heaved the bucket into the cockpit. I dropped the EPIRB into it. Bubbles rose, but nothing else happened. No lights or beeps. I yanked the EPIRB out of the water and shook it. Nothing. Disgusted, I threw it back into the bucket. Saltwater splashed all over, burning the deep cut on my shin.

I couldn't think clearly. My head throbbed and my body ached with every movement. There was nothing else I could think to do, short of jumping overboard and ending this nightmare. If Richard had beckoned, I would have jumped.

Don't, he could be alive.

"How in the hell can he be alive? Is he alive? Where is he?" I looked frantically in every direction. "Is he below? Is HE BELOW?" I shouted, expecting God to answer.

"WHERE IS HE? DOWN BELOW?" I struggled to get below as quickly as possible.

FOUR

Sinking

I fell down into a deep puddle. A good twenty inches of water covered the exposed bilge. "RICHARD, RICHARD," I bellowed. "WHERE ARE YOU?"

I knew he wasn't forward; I'd already been there, so I turned aft. Stumbling past the galley, throwing floating debris over my shoulders, I plowed into the aft cabin door that was hanging cockeyed off its hinges. I pushed and shoved and kicked, trying to get it out of my way, screaming, "RICHARD, RICHARD, I'M COMING I'LL HELP YOU. JUST WAIT, JUST WAIT. . . ."

The goddamn door wouldn't budge. I beat on it and rammed my body into it over and over and over. Finally things started falling away and the door fell backwards, creating its own tidal wave. I scrambled over it desperately searching—praying for Richard. I couldn't believe he wasn't in there. I looked in the aft head. I raised the toppled cushions. I even lifted the fallen door and ran my hand under the water to see if he was there.

"Oh why, why, why, didn't you come below?" In total despair I sank to my knees and became submerged in water up to my waist. I gasped and thought, My God, the boat's sinking, I've got to get out of here.

Struggling to lift my drenched, injured body, I staggered to the companionway and boosted myself up. Frantically I struggled to move the heavy life raft from the back of the cockpit to the middle of the boat, where I secured it to the cabin-top handrail. Instinctively I grabbed the rigging knife I kept on my belt, slid the sharp blade under a strap that held the raft shut, and started cutting upward. It was too tough—I was too weak. I resorted to hacking away at the straps.

As the last strap split, the life raft inflated and flung itself open. Inside I found fishing gear, hand flares, a miniature medical kit, a half dozen cans of water, and a sponge. Something was wrong, something was missing. I tried to think . . . fishing gear, flares, medical kit, sponge, food and water. Food? There's no food. There's cans of water but no opener for the cans. How can a life raft have no food and no way to open the water?

Going back over the boom, I banged the deep gash on my left shin. It started bleeding again. I ignored it. It was nothing compared to . . .

I went below to get food. Wading through the river, kicking everything in my way aside, I picked up a duffel bag.

Grabbing biscuits, cans of beans, tuna and peaches, I threw them into the bag. I took hold of the portable world band radio receiver and a can opener, and threw them in too. I pushed a blanket and a pillow up the companionway into the cockpit.

Water. I must have more water.

I looked around and saw the solar shower bag dangling from a shelf. It could hold two and a half gallons of water. "Richard will be thirsty when I find him," I said out loud. Grabbing the bag, I took it to the galley and began to fill it using the pressurized freshwater system. As the bag was filling, the stream of water started slowing down. It became a sputter, then a spit. "My God, I don't have any water!" Wait—the water filter's canister, there's bound to be at least a half gallon of water in it.

I pushed in the solar bag's stopper and struggled to get the heavy bag out the companionway. Slipping back down in the cabin, I took hold of the now full duffel bag and fought to get it topside. It weighed a ton, it tapped every ounce of strength I had.

I loaded the duffel bag and then the bedding into the life raft. As I was grabbing the solar bag, a swell hit *Hazana* broadside, causing her to roll. Everything in the raft tumbled overboard.

"NOT THE RADIO!" I screamed, as I watched the duffel bag sink and the bedding float away.

I couldn't stand it. I became a raving lunatic, stomping on the deck and kicking at the life raft. "THAT WAS STUPID,

STUPID. I'M SO STUPID. RICHARD, WHERE ARE YOU? YOU COME AND GET ME. DO YOU HEAR ME? YOU COME AND GET ME! GOD, YOU'VE GOT TO HELP ME!"

Wailing in utter frustration, I grabbed the solar bag and crawled inside the life raft, shaking with fear and futility, babbling, "I can't take it, Richard, I just can't take it. Why didn't you take me with you? You said, 'The captain goes down with the ship.' Remember? You said that! You lied to me. The ship did not go down. Where are you? How can I go on without you? What am I supposed to do? I don't know what to do. God, what should I do?"

"You never leave the ship," whispered Richard's soothing voice. He said it over and over, softly in my head. Hugging the water bag to my chest, I shut my eyes and sobbed, "But you left the ship, you left the ship." I cried myself to sleep in the rubber raft, not caring if the ship and I did sink.

FIVE

Currents and Drift

I woke up blubbering and freezing. I tried to open my crusty eyes. My neck and whole body felt stiff. I wanted desperately to keep sleeping, or die, so I wouldn't have to deal with this nightmare. The dawn was streaked with night's muddy black residue. I was chilled to the bone from a damp breeze that wouldn't stop licking my skin. I felt numb. The clanging of broken gear and the slap of water against the hull awoke all my fears again. I could barely move, my body ached merci-lessly. Each pang of pain left me breathless. I could barely swallow, my throat raw from screaming for Richard. Full of anger and defeat I grabbed a can of water out of the life raft and went below. Knowing I shouldn't drink the canned water yet, I pumped weak spurts of fresh water into my hand from the sink and slurped it, then licked my right palm. "Ugh, salty." I spit the saline residue out. Still thirsty, I opened the can of water—what the hell, I was just going to die anyway. I drank it all. It made me dizzy, it tasted horrible. All I wanted to do was lie back down and sleep until this horror went away.

Once in the aft cabin I swiped the books and clothes out of my way and then collapsed on the berth, shivering. I pulled a towel and some T-shirts over me and curled up in a ball, hugging Richard's broken guitar. There was a big hole in it. He would have hated that.

I woke up later to a door banging. I had been dreaming I was at a Victorian ball, dressed in a beautiful billowing affair, as were all the women. The men were in fancy costumes too. Renaissance music and long tables of food filled the room. The lighting had a yellow glow like candlelight, only brighter. Everyone was happy and gay, dancing around, eating and drinking. It was wonderful.

The door banged again. I yelled, "RICHARD, GET THE DOOR." Awakening, my heart froze. Oh, Richard, come back, please, come back. Richard . . .

I lay there and cried all over again. How could this happen? Why? We were so happy. . . . I started coughing and spit up blood. Oh God, what does this blood mean? Engulfed in loneliness and depression, I pretended Richard was there in the berth with me and I hugged the guitar tighter. I closed my eyes. The rise and fall of *Hazana* over the swells reminded me of riding the manta rays. Floating back into slumber, I drifted off and allowed myself to reminisce about the good times.

Richard at the helm of *Mayaluga*

The manta rays, that was a good time. . . .

We had anchored *Mayaluga* in Hakahetau Bay, on Ua Pou of the Marquesas Islands. A local named Luk invited us to go shark diving with him and some of his friends that night. I wasn't thrilled about the idea of shark diving, but not wanting to be left behind, I decided to go and just stay in the outrigger while the others dived.

Five of us went in two outriggers. The guys were using masks and snorkels, not air tanks, so they couldn't dive too deep or stay underwater too long. I saw Luk motion to Richard, and they both went down at the same time. All of a sudden I noticed their flashlights speed by, under the outrigger and beyond. After a few seconds, the lights headed for the surface, and Richard came bolting out of the water with Luk right behind him. I thought for sure a great white shark was on their tails. Swimming over to me Richard shouted, "You have to try this, love—we just rode a manta ray!"

Being content and safe in the outrigger, there was no way I was going in that shark-infested water. But after about a half hour of watching the guys have the time of their lives, I thought, Why not? I called Richard over and told him I was ready to try.

My stomach rose to my throat as I slid into the warm water. Richard and Luk swam over, and Luk motioned for me to stay close to him. Luk dove, and I dove right behind him. Below us was a huge black manta ray. Luk grabbed onto its fin, I grabbed onto Luk's leg, and off we went.

When I couldn't hold my breath any longer, I let go and watched Luk's light zip ahead as the manta swam away with its human cargo. Briefly alone, treading water, I turned my flashlight down toward the ocean floor. I could see nothing but my legs kicking. I looked up at the sky. The stars were brilliant. A whoop, then a light shining into my face drew my attention.

"Wasn't that incredible, love?" Richard asked.

"Totally amazing. Let's do it again!"

I woke up in *Hazana*'s aft cabin from my dream of manta ray–riding drenched with perspiration. My damp foul weather gear clung to my body. The air in the berth was dank. Condensation ran down the hull. The water in the boat lapped to *Hazana*'s rolling motion. The rhythmic banging and creaking wouldn't cease. Finally, I forced myself to get up.

I sloshed my way into the main salon; nothing had changed. The mess seemed to have grown. The nightmare remained. Stiff and aching all over, I climbed out of the cabin and rested in the cockpit. The sea was like a mammoth lake with swells barely distinguishable. In one sense I hated its flaccidity, for it should have been like this, not the ravaging monster it had become when Richard and I were trying to cross it. Now the sea is contrite, I observed, surreptitiously lurking around the world with its tail between its legs. I hawked a paltry, moistureless spit into the sea, then took hold of the binoculars and searched for my love again. There was nothing, nothing at all out there but the bloody glare of the sun off the water. Putting the binoculars down I succumbed to defeat and leaned back, letting the sun's warmth caress me. I didn't deserve this pleasure, yet I longed for warmth. With a mighty effort I peeled off my wet clothes. As each piece of clothing dropped off, the sun felt warmer and warmer, melting the icy crypt I was in. How can this feel so good when I feel so bad? It just didn't make sense.

I dozed until a fresh breeze woke me. I stared out to sea for a long time. The gleaming ocean tried to persuade me to be its friend again. "I hate you," flashed through my mind.

Turning and looking behind me, I saw nothing but a vast sheet of turquoise bleeding into an endless cobalt blue sky. No clouds, no whitecaps, no monstrous seas, no Richard. Just the sea and me.

I had to move. This was no good. There was so much I should be doing. Why was I alive? What did I live for? This?

What is this? A test? A test for what? Endurance? Torture? Had I been greedy in wanting all life has to offer? In wanting Richard? No. This is something else. What? I didn't know. God, what is this? Why?

Anxiety made me start shaking all over again. Take a deep breath, I told myself; feel the sun. I lay down and let the sun hit as much of my nude body as it could. I dozed, eventually waking up hot, covered with sweat, my head aching like it had been trapped in a vise.

You need to get the water out of the boat. The thought didn't force itself into my brain; it drifted in slowly, waiting to see if I'd accept it. I did. I got up and went into the dungeon.

It stunk. The beautiful tangerine and royal blue pareu Richard had bought me in Tahiti lay tangled in the hammock; I freed it and wrapped it around me. I stood there looking around, not knowing what to do.

You need to get the water out of the boat, said the voice in my mind again. I obeyed. I went over to the nav station and turned on the bilge-pump switch. Nothing happened. I knelt down and put my hand in the bilge water, thinking maybe I could feel if the external float switch had been fouled by some debris. As I touched it I got shocked. "OUCH!" I pulled my hand away. But if it was getting juice . . . I tentatively touched it once more and got zapped again.

I resorted to the manual bilge pump, but with all the debris in the water, its screen fouled quickly. I didn't have the strength to deal with it and gave up. Resting against the settee I stewed over the big job ahead—to get all this water out of the boat. *Hazana* didn't appear to be taking on any more water. I could slow down, I told myself—deal with it a little at a time.

Suddenly I noticed the exposed molded fiberglass of the cabin's ceiling. The Naugahyde-covered plywood sheets that used to cover the ceiling had fallen down and were strewn about. I got up and went into the V-berth. Digging through my backpack I found my rarely used lipstick. Back in the main salon I grabbed the sheets of liner and shoved them topside. I crawled up into the cockpit and wrote on each piece

HELP—I AM DEMASTED AT 15° N LAT

Each finished laminate was pushed overboard and stiffly undulated in the swells as it drifted with the current farther and farther away from me. Finally all five signs were cast out to sea, racing to find my rescuer. I would lose sight of them in the troughs, only to catch a glimpse as they crested the swells with their wet white vinyl reflecting my plum-colored plea to the heavens.

"What's the point? What's the bloody point?" I asked myself.

But then that strange little voice in my head, the voice that was becoming my friend, my savior, mysteriously butted in. *Don't give up, love. Don't give up.*

Was it Richard? It didn't sound like Richard.

You need to get this boat moving, the voice softly hinted.

"Leave me alone."

Why don't you eat something?

"Why don't you?"

Okay, I will.

The voice's invisible hands gently pulled me up by my armpits. I went below. The mess made me nauseous. "Forget it," I said aloud, my voice sounding strange. Weak and exhausted, I rested against the counter in the galley.

EAT! The voice startled me. I looked around uneasily. No one was there. In the sink I saw a jar of peanut butter. Even though I didn't feel hungry, I grabbed the jar and tried to open it. I couldn't get the lid off. I knew that voice would scream at me if I didn't try harder, so I banged the lid of the jar on the counter. The sound reverberated in my head. The lid opened. I found a spoon in the upheaval and dug out an oily scoop, setting the open jar on the galley counter.

"Go ahead, fall off, I could care less." I addressed the innocent container of peanut butter: "Why aren't you already broken anyway?" When the jar stayed put, I directed my attention to the manual bilge pump. I strained to give it a couple of pumps, then licked at the spoon. The peanut butter stuck to my tongue like a snail to concrete. I allowed my mouth to suck hard while I pictured a shell-less slug being crushed to death, like the wave that came down on . . . *Stop it!*

A forceful scrape across the hull startled me to my feet. "YOU STOP IT." I screamed like a crazy woman. "I'LL SHOW YOU!" And like a bulldozer I plowed back to the aft cabin, where I hunted and dug around until I found the big wire cutters. With spoon in mouth and wire cutters in hand, I crawled up to the cockpit.

Once topside I had to rest; repeatedly climbing in and out

of the boat and carrying the heavy wire cutters had exhausted me. I pulled the spoon out of my mouth and threw it overboard, barking, "You drown too." The blob of peanut butter left in my mouth was thick and dense, not good or bad. I knew by my eating it the voice would shut up. Richard loved peanut butter and I moaned remembering that. I hoped he had found something to eat by now too.

An obnoxious *bang-scraaaccck-clunk* sound once again sent an angry rush through me. "THAT'S IT," I threatened. "YOU ARE OUT OF HERE!" I shouted toward the stern of the boat, snapping the wire cutters frantically. I needed to calm down and come up with a logical order for getting rid of the stainless steel wires and rigging that were dragging through the water and holding the mizzenmast against the hull, banging and scraping, driving me crazy. It was a hazard to *Hazana*. One solid bash could puncture a hole in the side of the boat.

I went aft and started with the mizzenmast. I spent a long time trying to cut free the three-eighth-inch stainless steel shroud. My muscles felt weak and strained—atrophied. I wanted desperately to quit. But who would do this if I didn't? I twisted and sawed and clamped and crunched the big wire cutters. Slowly the threads of steel unraveled and split. With the final cut, the mizzenmast sank and *Hazana* regained some of her composure. But my composure, what little I had left, failed me. I desperately hoped this was the right thing to do. For I could never recapture the rig if I suddenly realized I needed it later.

It was the right thing to do. You couldn't lift all that weight on board. It was a hazard bashing into the hull, the voice assured me.

There was still the roller-furling jib and staysail, trailing in the water off the bow. Sails! If only I were strong enough to get them on board. I went to the bow and stared at the sails in the water. There was no way to save the jib, it would take twenty he-men to lift it on board. So I pulled the clevis pin that was holding it and watched the sail free itself from the staysail and slowly diminish in size as *Hazana* drifted forward with the current.

With nothing to lose, and possibly a lot to gain, I tried to haul in the staysail. It was sopping wet, holding tons of water in its folds. I could barely lift it an inch.

"I can't do it. I just can't." With no winch and no muscle, I gave up and pulled its clevis pin too, then sat down on the deck, crying and sobbing as the staysail floated away in the water. I had desperately hoped it would be helping me sail to land.

Hazana liked not being encumbered by her fouled rigging and I liked the freshened breeze. Tears weren't solving anything.

Standing up, I staggered back to the cockpit and went below. The nav station was a mess, littered with books and broken glass. I wiped the glass off the seat and sat down. Taking hold of the VHF radio's microphone, I called for help: "Mayday. Mayday. Mayday. Does anybody hear me?" Nothing.

"Damn thing." As I let go of the mike it sprung back

across the chart table. Why should I hang it up properly? It was broken like everything else.

Putting my hand to my forehead, I felt a burn from the gash. *You better look at that cut,* the voice whispered.

"I don't want to." But I got up and went to the head anyway. It wasn't me I stared at in the mirror, it was some freak. I could see layers of skin inside the deep gash. "My brain is oozing out. Good," I said without much conviction.

I dug the medical kit out from inside the cabinet, and set it down on the closed lid of the commode. As I searched through it, I found a vial of morphine. I picked it up and looked at it, mesmerized. Then I looked at the freak in the mirror.

No, Tami. Don't even think about it, came the voice.

"Why not?" I challenged.

Because if you were meant to die, you would have.

"I wish I would have."

I know.

To kill myself would be against everything I had been taught in my life. If Richard drowned he was meant to—this was a realization I was beginning to allow to creep into my consciousness. At least Richard died admirably, doing what he loved, and there was the slight chance he could still be alive. The "Ohmigod" could have been screamed out of seeing a vision of the Almighty in the wave, the water. Couldn't it? Perhaps I misinterpreted it. It could have been awe, not terror, but awe.

I carefully put the vial back in the medical bag, placed the bag back in the cabinet, and slammed the door shut. Opening the rubbing alcohol I had found, I poured some on a washcloth and pressed it to my forehead, then screeched, "DAMN IT, DAMN IT, DAMN IT," for the antiseptic burned like hell. "OH GOD," I pleaded, "take me home, please take me home to Richard."

There were sutures on board, but I couldn't bring myself to sew my head shut. Instead, I drew the skin together as tightly as I could tolerate and put several large butterfly bandages on the long wound. Pus and blood oozed out. It was disgusting. To recapture some semblance of cleanliness, I carefully dabbed at the cuts on my arms and legs with the burning alcohol. It hurt, but not nearly as much as the thought of how Richard must hurt.

I found a bandanna in the V-berth and pulled my tangled hair up, wrapping the cloth around my head. I leaned against the berth, hating myself for not being able to commit suicide. I didn't know what to do; there was so much to do.

Check the chart. Make a plan to get to land.

Begrudgingly I got up and aimed for the nav station. If I was going to live, let's get to living. And maybe, just maybe, Richard would be my reward at the end of this.

At the nav station, I found the chart we'd been using that showed our last known position plotted on it and the logbook. I squinted, forcing the last words Richard wrote into focus: "Bloody Raymond now going WEST again. 140 knots still. All we can do is pray."

"Oh why weren't our prayers answered?" I whimpered. "Why? I should just go jump overboard and . . ."

You should finish what you started—make a plan to get to land.

I dug around in the nav station drawer for a pen and boldly wrote in the logbook, "Hit by Hurricane Raymond." Then crumbled into sobs again. "It's okay, it's okay," I finally said to myself, grabbing a hand towel that was haphazardly dangling from the oven implanted in the bookshelf along the hull above my head. I wiped my face dry. With a deep breath I forced myself to concentrate as best I could and went over and over the path Richard and I had traveled from Tahiti. It was so hard to concentrate.

I can't be that far from the accident, can I? I looked at the clock—let's see, I came to, what, two—three days ago? Two, I thought. Glancing down at the chart, I picked up the plotting tools and started to calculate. I decided Cabo San Lucas must be about twelve hundred miles to the northeast, and Hilo, Hawaii, approximately fifteen hundred miles to the northwest. I calculated this repeatedly on the chart, writing down numbers and degrees over and over. I'd be better off going with the trades and currents to Hawaii. That heading would be about three hundred degrees on the compass.

But Cabo is closer to home.

I have no home without Richard.

You have many homes. You have your mom's home and your dad's home. You have your grandma and grandpa's home.

"Is Richard home?"

Yes, Richard is home. Now, you go home via Hawaii; it makes the most sense.

"What do you mean, Richard is home?" Silence. The only sound in my brain was its own buzzing. "WHAT DO YOU MEAN, RICHARD IS HOME?" I yelled.

The voice wouldn't answer.

"WELL THEN, GO TO HELL, VOICE," I screamed. To spite the voice I went to the sink, where I cranked the handle on the faucet and waited through each airy sputter as a cup filled with water. Then I drank greedily, even licking the last drops.

You already had four ounces of water.

"BE QUIET!" I yelled, glancing at the water gauge, which read empty. Filled with guilt, I threw the cup down. Going over to a berth I grabbed a sleeping bag, Richard's flowered shirt and his guitar, and pushed it all topside, leaving the morbid dungeon.

Vowing never to go below again, I made a bed in the cockpit and lashed the wheel to keep the rudder straight. This would help *Hazana* make as much headway as possible with the current.

I started rocking back and forth, back and forth. At some point I picked up Richard's guitar and started strumming and singing.

I put the guitar down, crawled into the sleeping bag, and pulled it tightly around me.

"Good night, love," I uttered to the star-filled sky.

Good night yourself, love, the voice ever so lightly whispered back.

SIX

Jury Rig

My face felt on fire. I opened my eyes only to be blinded by the sun. "Not another day," I moaned.

Come on, Tami. Get up. Eat something. Get this boat moving.

The voice was scary, yet comforting too. It always seemed to know what to do, or what I should do. Actually, it was many voices. Sometimes it sounded like my mother, or my father, or Richard. But mostly it sounded like me.

I went below, found another spoon, and filled it with peanut butter because it was easy. Back in the sun, I sat sporadically licking my spoon and trying to figure out how to get *Hazana* moving. The spinnaker pole caught my eye. If I put it on end, it could act as a mast. It was still lashed down on the foredeck. About six feet of it had been sheared off when the mainmast broke and fell over.

I walked up to the bow and peered into the anchor-chain locker. It was about three feet deep. I moved back and unlashed the nine-foot spinnaker pole and stuck it down in the hole.

The purpose of a spinnaker pole is to hold out one of the largest sails a boat can fly—a spinnaker—while sailing downwind. The spinnaker pole stood only about six feet in the air. With so little height, I shook my head and said, "This is ridiculous."

It's not ridiculous.

"How am I going to fill a sail with wind if the pole's only six feet in the air?"

Fill up the chain locker so the pole's higher in the air.

"You fill it up."

Okay, gladly.

As I laid the pole on the deck to go below, the strange force establishing itself in me silently directed me to lash the pole back down to the deck in case a swell tempted it to roll overboard. Could the voice be like a guardian angel? That was a weird thought.

Why is it a weird thought?

"I don't know. . . ."

In the V-berth, I opened the hatch and pushed all the pillows and blankets out onto the bow, plus anything else that would fill up the chain locker. Then I crawled out of the hatch and shut it behind me.

I crammed all the objects into the chain locker I had pushed topside. I unlashed the spinnaker pole and then stood it up in the locker. The pole reached a full nine feet into the air. This gave me the first sense of well-being I had felt since I came to. Something was finally being accomplished. I lashed the pole back onto the deck before I went back to the cockpit.

"You're the last sail I've got," I said out loud to the storm jib. "You're the miracle sail. How did you not get swept overboard? The propane tanks got ripped out of their locker and the deck was wiped clean, but you stayed in the cockpit without even being tied down. Why didn't Richard? Why didn't *you* get ripped off this boat instead and have the life sucked out of you?"

I dropped the storm jib and grabbed my stomach, bending over in pain.

Don't think about it. TAMI—don't think about it. It's over. It's over now. You'll be okay. You'll make it. Richard's at peace.

"Richard's dead. I know he's dead. I'll never see him again."

It was quick. Quick.

What did the stupid voice know? Angrily, I questioned: "Quicker than what's going to happen to me?" Not expecting or wanting a reply, I grabbed the sail and dragged it to the bow, securing it under the spinnaker pole.

I went down into the aft cabin to collect the rigging blocks I had discovered under a bunk.

Back on the bow, I rested a minute, and in my mind I recalled the dynamics of a rigged mainmast. There were the headstay and the backstay. They secured the mast straight up from the bow and stern directions. Then there were the shrouds. They ran from the masthead to the deck, on both sides of the boat. All this rigging, the stays and the shrouds, were to hold a mast upright and plumb. "Okay, that's right," I mumbled to myself, irritated that I had to concentrate so hard on what used to come so naturally.

I contemplated how the leading edge of a sail, in its normal position, attaches to a mast. But my mast—the spinnaker pole—was short, a mere nine feet in the air. If I took the shortest side of the sail and attached it tautly to the spinnaker pole, then tied two other lines—sheets—to the sail, so I could pull the sail to whichever side of the boat I needed it to be on in order to collect wind, it should work.

I went ahead with my plan. I attached a line from the top of the pole to a fitting on the bow, and secured a second line from the top of the pole to a pad eye on the deck. This held the pole fore and aft. Next I rigged the shrouds, to keep the pole from falling sideways.

I pulled the storm jib out of its bag and rolled it out. I was afraid it would blow overboard even though there wasn't much wind, so I clipped it down and secured it as I continued. Once the sail was laid out, I ran a line from what would normally be the head of the sail, but now would be the clew, through a block to a winch in the cockpit. This would act as my sheet. I could sit in the cockpit and tighten or loosen the sail, depending on Mother Nature's whim and the amount of wind that matched her mood.

I rigged a block at the top of the spinnaker pole, then ran a line through that block and attached one end to what would normally be the clew but would now be the head of the sail. The other end of the line I led to the anchor windlass. This created the halyard to my jury rig, allowing me to lower and raise the sideways rigged sail. I used the anchor windlass as my winch to keep the luff, or forward edge, of the sail taut.

I spent a whole day creating the rig and adjusting the lines that served as stays and shrouds. I then relocated the blocks and shackles in search of the proper angle that produced the most sail area. Finally, I hauled the sail up the pole and secured the halyard. I went back into the cockpit and adjusted the sheet. The sail was slow to fill, but she did. She carried only about forty-five square feet of sail area, but that was forty-five square feet more than I had had two days before. I finally felt something different from pain. I felt hope. "We're flying, *Hazana*. Pushing two knots, I'd bet. Way to go, girl."

Good job, Tami.

"Thank you. Thank you, thank you, thank you," I said to the great emptiness. When the voice didn't respond, my enthusiasm faded. I needed that voice; it was becoming The Voice, the only thing for me to communicate with. It was more than me talking to myself, it was outside of me, yet in me. I needed The Voice's approval.

Even if the pace was only a knot or two an hour, it felt exhilarating. At least I was making way with some control of my direction. Besides, I knew if I didn't get home my mom would never, ever, stop looking for me. I was all she really had since my parents divorced when I was young—an infant. Did my mother feel this desolate when my father left? She couldn't have—their choice to divorce was mutual. I was never offered a choice. No one asked me if Richard could leave—he just left, disappeared. It might as well have been divorce. But he didn't want to leave me. He loved me and I loved him. "Oh God, how I loved him. I can't do this."

You can do anything you put your mind to, The Voice insisted.

It sounded just like my mom. She had said that I could do anything too. Anything I had the guts to try. How's this, Mom? Did you ever think I'd have the guts to try to survive all alone out here in the back of beyond? With no answer in the wind, I took a deep sigh and pulled on the line, tightening my newly created rig. I looked at the compass and turned the wheel slightly to the three-hundred-degree course I hoped would get me to Hawaii. Then I bowed my head and cried, for I had no one, not a soul in this vast, watery, whole wide world but me.

SEVEN

Time on My Hands

"Mayday. Mayday. Mayday. This is the sailing vessel *Hazana*. Isn't there one bloody person out there?" I said, staring at the microphone in my hand.

The sound of static was maddening. I tried again: "Mayday. Mayday. Mayday. This is the sailing yacht *Hazana*. Does anybody hear me? Over."

The antenna had been attached to the top of the mainmast. With the mainmast gone, there was no antenna. I could see the coaxial cable traveling overhead in the cabin to where the mainmast had been. I pulled out what was left of the severed cable and led it out the companionway to one of the standing stanchions. Cutting the short antenna off the EPIRB, I taped its center wire to the raw end of the coaxial cable and then maydayed again but still heard only static. I figured it had been four days since the hurricane, which put the date at October 15. In the logbook I wrote, "Someone please tell me this is all a bad dream."

To stay sane, I moved to the manual bilge pump for a while. About every hour I would send out a mayday, but there were so many hours of emptiness, of feeling lonely and scared, and as much as I wanted to I was unable to sleep. I sat at the wheel, steering, keeping *Hazana* on course. I thought and thought and thought. I thought again about my parents, my grandparents, and my younger brother. How if I had followed in my mother's footsteps I'd already have a child in school and I wouldn't be in this mess. I'd be safe and sound at home.

Yes, but you wouldn't have met Richard.

"I might still have met Richard. And he would still have loved me, even if I did have a child."

But would you have taken your child out of school to go sailing?

I could have home-schooled on the boat. Or maybe my mom would have watched the child, like my grandparents watched me.

Do you think the child would have resented your leaving?

"No, why? I certainly didn't resent my mother having me live with my grandparents for a few years. They spoiled me. They absolutely loved me to death."

What an odd phrase—"loved me to death." Keep remembering how much they all love you, Tami, they love you to life.

"They love me to life. Well, they all certainly encouraged me to live my dream. Boy, if they could see me now. Some dream! A friggin' nightmare!"

My thoughts, as always, returned to Richard. We had had so many plans; how could it have ended like this? It just didn't make any sense. What about "God is good," and all that? What was good about this? Richard had been good. I'd been good. I just didn't get it. And there was no one to talk to, to help me understand. No one to share this grief with. No shoulder to cry on except the curve of Richard's guitar. I strummed the guitar lightly. At least it was a sound other than the waves slapping against the hull and the small shuffle of the awkwardly hoisted sail. I stared at the water and felt Richard all around me. If only he'd appear and hold me and make it all right as he had in the past.

I grabbed Richard's flowered shirt I so loved on him and squeezed it to my chest. As I rocked myself to sleep I thought of how I knew where Richard was; he was in my heart, but where was I? Perhaps tomorrow, at the blush of the morn, I'd find out. Day's first light often has revealed good boons— good things to come.

⸻

The day broke clear and warm, with *Hazana* moving like a rocking horse in very slow motion. If the weather held, it would be a perfect day for my sun sights. The sextant hadn't broken in the capsize, which was a miracle. It had been in its case, lashed down on a shelf at the nav station. Being the delicate instrument it is, the sextant helps the mariner locate a position by using two objects to measure altitudes above sea level. My two objects were the horizon line and the sun.

By looking through the sight tube and adjusting the index arm, the sun is seen through a series of mirrors. When the arm is adjusted properly, the sun appears to tap the horizon line. That time is immediately marked down, along with the degrees that correspond on the sextant's index. The mariner then looks up the data in the book of tables to establish a position.

It's important to have exact time when taking a sun sight. My stopwatch was ruined in the capsize and I didn't have a clue as to what had happened to my wristwatch. Only the clock in the main cabin, mounted on the bulkhead, remained to help me mark the moment the sun's lower edge would tap the horizon. But the bulkhead clock was too far away to document the exact time. Therefore, I could only find my latitudinal position in the Pacific, but gaining that knowledge gave me something to look forward to. Finding my latitude would be exciting yet intimidating, for what if I'd been way off and I was already halfway to China?

Taking the sun sight promised to be tricky. The broken boom blocking the companionway would take seconds away from seeing the exact time. I was going to have to peer through the sight tube, carefully set the fragile sextant down, and then lean way over the boom into the companionway so that I could see the clock on the bulkhead and note the exact time as precisely as possible. I sat in the warm cockpit, recalling the basics of celestial navigation, and eagerly waited for noon.

When learning celestial navigation, I had had certain

facts ingrained in me. I knew my chance of catching the sun at the exact second it reached its highest point in the sky, its zenith, was not that important, for the sun hangs at its zenith for about two minutes. It's fairly easy to predict these two minutes by going into the navigation tables and figuring the zenith time mathematically. With the noon sight, I could try to identify where I was—at least know the latitude. My tentative plan was to reach the northern nineteenth latitude, turn left and, hopefully, reach Hawaii. The big island, Hawaii, stretches between latitude 19° N and 20° N, and being set to the north as I headed west, I figured, should put me somewhere in the middle of the island, where Hilo is located. As noon approached, I became excited. I sat straddling the boom, looking at the clock below, waiting for the second hand to hit the 12. The moment it did, I located the sun through the sextant and took my first reading. I carefully set the sextant down in its padded box and held on to the boom as I hung upside down to see the clock. 1201 hours.

Climbing off the boom, I repeated, "1201, 1201," and went down below to the nav station. I opened the *1983 Nautical Almanac,* the book that would give me all the information I needed to plot my position, and methodically did my calculations. It was October 16, Day Five after the capsize. My sight gave me a latitudinal position of 18° N. This was astonishing news. I was much farther north than I had imagined. I glanced at the clock. There was no kink to its second hand, just its steady jump—one-thousand-one, one-thousand-two—

but I was filled with doubt. What if the clock had stopped for a while and then started again? How could I be sure my latitude position was 18° N?

"If the clock is wrong, it'll screw everything up. If I'm too far south, I could miss all the Hawaiian islands and end up in China or some other Far Eastern port," I said out loud.

"Forget it, I'm just going to trust my sun sight and head for nineteen degrees north, hang a left, and hope I don't miss Hawaii."

Anxiously I picked up the mike and maydayed again. Nothing. I glanced over at the galley sink; I was dying of thirst. I desperately wanted a drink of water, but I knew I had to ration. It was too soon to have more. But before I could stop myself, I had jumped up and grabbed a cup, filled it with water from the hand pump and downed it.

You're only stealing from yourself, girl.

Guilt-ridden, I shouted, "I DON'T CARE. I HAD TO HAVE SOME." Throwing the cup down in the sink, I raced away from the nagging voice to the fresh air.

Sitting at the wheel, the boat bobbing like a toy in a tub, nothing along the horizon, I let myself daydream. I remembered how Richard and I always loved the idea of being the only boat in a bay. Like when we went to Fatu Hiva, in the Marquesas.

Fatu Hiva has only two charted villages. Most sailors go into Hanavave, the Bay of Virgins, because it has a better

Sailing into the South Pacific on *Mayaluga*

anchorage. But Richard and I went into Omoa Bay to get off the beaten path and experience unspoiled Polynesian culture. As we approached Omoa Bay, huge stone pinnacles thrust up into the sky like sentinels guarding their village. With the anchor barely set and the sails stowed, we watched as an outrigger loaded with fresh fruit pulled up next to the boat.

"Bonjour. Ça va?"

"Pas mal. Et toi?" Richard cheerfully replied.

"Ça va, ça va!! Je m'appelle Jon. Et toi?"

"Moi c'est Richard, et ça c'est mon amie, Tami."

While they carried on in French, of which I could only pick up bits and pieces, I studied Jon and his mild manner. He was slender, of medium height, with stomach muscles like a washboard. He had the local dark eyes, dark hair, and dark skin. His face was extremely friendly and his smile bright.

Jon gave us a big sack of *pamplemousse* (grapefruit), oranges, and papayas. He noticed our diminishing stock of bananas hanging from the boom crutch.

"What do you think, Tami?" Richard asked me. "Would you like to go to Jon's house later to meet his family and replenish our banana supply?"

"I'd love to."

Richard mapped out a plan to meet Jon later in the afternoon on the beach.

Even though I couldn't speak Marquesan and only knew a little French that I had learned during my last voyage through the South Pacific, I knew that trading is big sport—an art, an art of finesse. The locals, being naturally generous, expect nothing in return. The art is to learn to be naturally generous yourself and not appear to trade because you feel you owe it, but rather because you love to give.

We had brought along trading stock: backpacks, flip-flops, thread in all colors, perfume, baseball caps, crayons, coloring books, and baby clothes. A locker on board had been designated just for these goods. We loaded our backpacks with T-shirts, a baseball cap, and perfume and rowed ashore. We met Jon on the beach and followed him through the small village, passing houses and bungalows. The houses were made of cinder block or wood with corrugated aluminum roofs. Occasionally, we'd see a thatched roof. The yards around the houses were not manicured, just leveled brush cut back away from the structure. Beyond these yards, the lush jungle prevailed, with indescribable beauty. Everyone appeared to contribute to the self-sufficiency of the village.

One family made bread; another raised chickens. One family built an addition onto their house and stocked it with the odd canned goods, shelf cheese, and boxed milk. It was the local store.

Jon's front porch was cheerfully painted white and turquoise. A stream ran down alongside the house. Banana and fruit trees grew in abundance right in the front yard. We met Mareva, Jon's wife, and their two children: Taupiri, a five-year-old boy, and Lovinea, an infant girl. Mareva was a stunning, tall Marquesan woman in her late twenties. She had silky long black hair and arresting black eyes, a real beauty.

Mareva invited us into the house. After we shooed the chickens off the table and moved the baskets of breadfruit and taro to one side, we sat down. Jon joined us as Mareva served coffee in soup bowls with a spoon. "Taofe," Jon announced, pointing to the bowls of coffee. Sweetened condensed milk was passed around. We watched Jon to see how to drink our taofe. He generously poured the milk in until his taofe looked like melted vanilla ice cream. The islanders seemed to use the sweetened condensed milk everywhere—on bread, in their taofe, and in their babies' bottles. Unfortunately, the locals' love of the sweet milk as well as sugar and fruit caused massive tooth decay, as evidenced by their wide, gaping smiles. Mareva served fish, bread, and salad. It was delicious.

We finished our meal and followed Jon out to the stream running alongside the house to wash our faces and hands. The wind was freshening, and I could see that Richard was getting concerned about *Mayaluga*. I decided this would be a good time to break out our trading stash. Reaching inside my backpack, I pulled out some baby clothes. When I handed them to Mareva, her eyes grew as big as saucers. She held them up and gave me her sparse-toothed grin. I also had brought a dress and perfume and thread, as well as a T-shirt for her son. I felt like one of Santa's elves as we rowed back out to *Mayaluga*.

The next morning we awoke early. Jon had promised to take us into the hills to the tapa man. We knew tapas are made from the bark of mulberry, breadfruit, or banyan trees. It is pounded thin into strong canvases and cloths of all sizes and shapes.

After hiking for some time, we came to a clearing. In front of us was what looked like a thatched treehouse. But as we approached, I could see that one end of the floor rested on low pillars dug into the side of the hill, and that the other end was secured with two-by-fours to coconut trees. The walls of the house were made with palm fronds, and the roof was rusty corrugated aluminum.

Below the treehouse, in a level clearing, three women sat beating tree bark with short, baseball bat–like sticks against the trunk of a fallen coconut tree. We startled them, and they quit beating and smiled demurely. Jon approached and spoke to them in Marquesan. During his conversation he turned and pointed to us. We nodded and smiled. The oldest woman pointed to the thatched hut and nodded, and Jon waved at us to follow him up the path.

The front door was square and only about four feet high; we had to bend down to enter. Inside, the hut was dimly lit, even though two large glass windows were open. An old man in tattered shorts sat hunched, painting a tapa spread on a large table located in the corner of the twenty-by-twenty-foot hut. "Ia orana" (Good day), said Jon, causing the old man to look up.

"Maeva" (Welcome), the frail grandfather said, as he got up and came over to Jon and kissed both his cheeks.

Jon introduced us to Henry, who kissed our cheeks too.

Henry's hunched back and weary eyes indicated he had led a strenuous life. He waved us over to his worktable, where a two-by-four-foot piece of tapa lay. I noticed this tapa was coarser and thicker, different from the supple tapa the Samoans and Tongans make for clothing. Henry had painted symbols and figures on the tapa with black ink made from local roots. The pictures on tapas depict a statement and/or tell a story.

From an old trunk, Henry brought out many tapas to select from. We chose five we liked. From our backpacks, we pulled out trading items. He wanted to trade a backpack and a pair of flip-flops. We finally convinced him to take some money as well.

We said good-bye to Henry and walked back down the path to where the women were methodically pounding out the cloth. The older woman was Henry's wife, Jon told us, and the two girls, his daughters. The girls kept looking at me and giggling. I smiled at them and asked Richard why he thought they were laughing—was it something I had done? Richard asked Jon and then explained to me that the youngest girl would like to touch my hair.

"Really?" I said, surprised. "Sure." I motioned for her to come over.

The girl appeared to be in her mid-teens, and was so shy that she would hardly look me in the eye. I leaned my head over to make it easier for her to take hold of and rub my long blond hair between her fingers. She glanced at her sister with a smile. I motioned for the sister to come over too.

The sister promptly came over, gently rubbed my hair, and said, "Henehe."

In French, Jon said, "La belle," to Richard.

"Yes, beautiful," repeated Richard, proudly looking into my eyes.

I smiled at him and then at the girls, thinking how odd it must be for the young Marquesans to see blond hair. Their own thick, black hair was also waist long, but tied back and much shinier than mine.

I reached into my backpack and pulled out some lipstick and perfume.

"Un pour vous, et un pour vous," I said to the girls. Before the sisters would take the gifts, their eyes pleaded with their mother. She nodded yes to them.

"Merci, Madame," each girl quietly said to me, switching to French.

"Il n'y a pas de quoi" (It was nothing), I replied, pleased with my growing French vocabulary.

I smiled and stared at the women; thinking how exotic they looked in this remote and tropical setting. It was so peaceful and serene.

My eyes drifted from the sea to the wrecked deck of *Hazana*. How wonderful it would have been to have some women friends here to talk to—anyone, Richard. This fifth day had warmed to scorching hot without a breath of wind. *Hazana* floundered and I floundered with her.

"Voice, are you there?" I ventured.

Silence.

"I'm sorry I stole the water."

Think twice next time.

"Okay."

The next morning out of boredom I went below to straighten things up. The depression felt bottled up in me. I grabbed the pen and wrote in the logbook: "I'm very, very distraught." I closed my eyes and felt my heart starting to beat faster and faster. Maybe I'll have a heart attack and drop dead, I thought.

Distract yourself, The Voice suggested. *You were going to straighten things up, remember?*

Looking around the main cabin, I didn't know where to begin. This used to have such an elegant interior, with its luxurious upholstery, spotless overhead liner, and polished woodwork. I carefully made my way to the V-berth, thinking I should start forward and work my way aft. I couldn't believe how many things that belonged in the main cabin and galley were now crammed up in the V-berth. I knew we had capsized, but with this much damage and the way things were heaved about the cabin I knew we had to have pitchpoled too—flipped end over end, like a gymnast sprightly executing a handspring on a mat.

I came across an oar. Perhaps I could use this to flag down a boat, I thought, but how would it stand out against the drab sea? I glanced around and then remembered a red T-shirt of Richard's that said, "Bay Scuba—Our business is going under." I tied it around the oar's blade. Red, the color of love—the color of blood.

Red, the color of rescue, chimed in The Voice.

I tossed the oar up into the cockpit.

Forcing myself to keep cleaning, I tackled mopping up the grunge out of the bilge. I filled a bucket with saltwater and found a sponge. As I mopped under a floorboard around a floor frame, something scraped against the ragged fiberglass hull. I pinched the object with the large sponge and pulled it out. My God, it was my wristwatch. How in the hell did it get in there? This was a godsend. I dunked the watch in the bucket of saltwater and, with forefinger and sponge, rubbed the grunge off it. Staring at it, I watched the seconds tick. 0933 hours I read on its face. I glanced at the clock on the bulkhead, noting its time of 0935 hours. Deeply cheered, I burst out loud, "I can pinpoint my exact position now that I can cross my morning sight with my afternoon sight." I dropped the sponge in the bucket, went over to the nav station and grabbed a pencil and paper. I took the sextant out of its box. This and the watch were my lifelines to land. I tenderly carried them topside.

Straddling the boom, I located the sun through the sextant. I slowly pulled the release on the sextant's arm, which lowered the mirrored image of the sun down in the lens to the horizon. I pushed the lap-time button on the wristwatch. Then I swung the sextant side-to-side, just enough to get the bottom of the sun to skim the horizon line. When I observed the bottom of the sun tap the horizon line, I took a mark by stopping the watch. The recorded time read 0954 and 27 seconds. I looked where the arrow pointed on the arc of the sextant and wrote down the degrees. Then I did the whole procedure again, taking a total of three marks. These three marks would give me a choice of the reading I felt most accurately marked the moment the sun hit the horizon.

I took the watch, sextant, and paperwork below and calculated with the *1983 Nautical Almanac* and the sight reduction tables my LOP—line of position. With the calculations completed, I plotted my LOP on the plotting sheet. "Well," I said to myself, "I'm somewhere on this line."

Near noon I eagerly did the whole thing over again. This sight would be "the fix," the sight that would tell me exactly where I was.

I found myself to be on longitude 134° W by latitude 18° N. This was good news. I no longer had to speculate on my position. I was closer to Hawaii than I had thought.

I was eager for Day Eight to arrive so I could take my sights again and see how far I had gone during the night.

As the day opened calm, I wasn't needed at the wheel. To keep my mind off Richard I went below and got back to my cleaning chores. Much to my joy I came across the mizzen staysail. The mizzen staysail would be better in the light air than the storm jib I had raised. It might fit the jury rig better, I hoped.

It was a challenge to push the mizzen staysail's dead weight out of the forehatch and drag it to the foredeck. I had gone below to get more lines, when suddenly the boat heeled. Oh no, I thought and quickly scrambled topside to find the mizzen staysail overboard, slowly sinking into the sea.

No, no, no. Damn it. Will I ever learn? I ranted and raved. Then I sat down and cried.

You have to stop crying, Tami.

"Shut up."

You need that water; you're getting dehydrated.

"Just shut up. They're my tears and I'll cry if I want to!" I yelled, then tittered, as the song with those words came to mind and I remembered that it dealt with a party. Some party this was.

But I knew The Voice was right. I had so little water left. Crying would not help.

"I could drink saltwater," I challenged The Voice.

It'll make you crazy.

"I already am crazy."

You might be, but you're not stupid.

"I just let the sail roll off the boat, and that's pretty stupid."

Well, I bet you won't do that again.

"You're right, because I don't have another sail."

Maybe you should be happy you have the storm jib and get on with your first sight of the day.

Conceding, I wiped the tears from my face with my fingers and licked the tiny drops. With a deep breath I stared at the storm jib hanging limp on the erect pole. What was the point? Maybe I should just roll off this boat like the mizzen staysail and be done with it. But I was eager to do my first sun sight of the day. I looked at my watch; it was almost 0900. I went below and got the pencil, paper, and sextant.

My first sight looked good.

But my noon sight threw me. I calculated 132° W by 18° 11" N. I had lost two degrees of longitude! That's what, 120 miles? It was like I had gone backwards in the night. What happened? I wasn't as far west as I thought. Everything was going wrong. I sat at the wheel, fuming. Disillusioned, my mind and body gave in to all its aches and pains.

At 0200 I did my third sight of the day. Yep, two degrees off. To ease my frustration I opened a can of sweet peaches and spent hours nibbling on each slick, copper spear of fruit. To hell with peanut butter.

EIGHT

Water Above, Water Below

It had turned cold. I put on jeans and a foul-weather jacket and went back to sitting at the wheel, steering as I had been doing for the past couple of days. I spent most of that time, after eating the sweet peaches, trying to remember why it had been so important for Richard to stay topside and not come below with me before the capsize. Had I known that would be the last time I would ever see him, the last touch of his skin, the last grin, the last glowing wink of love, I would have flown out of the companionway and into his arms. I would have clasped onto him like a giant octopus does its prey and fervently torpedoed to the bottom of the ocean with him in one last orgasmic roll. We could have died in each other's arms, defying love until death do us part.

It was now Day Eleven. No ships in sight. No one answering my maydays. No miracles. Sporadically I'd maneuver the manual bilge pump and feel the pressure of water being sucked out of the bilge as I pulled the lever up, and then plunged into the sea as I forced the lever down. I pictured the grungy stream of water as it exploded out of its through-hull fitting into the vast sparkling sea. The mixed molecules and particles of pain, blood, food, and debris, finally set free to dissipate into the now stabilized Pacific Ocean. How could I suck myself through the fitting and be set free?

It didn't dawn on me until the clouds were overhead to consider the old salt's saying: "Red sky in morning, sailor take warning." Red sky in mourning . . .

As the first gust of wind slapped my cheek and the ominous black clouds spit rain in my face, I began to shake uncontrollably. A storm was about to break. Adrenaline pumped through me, fear squeezed from every pore, and I reacted in desperation. I buckled the EPIRB back on my waist, forgetting it didn't work, and strapped on my safety harness, clipping the tether to the binnacle. I examined the D-ring. Could it freakishly part too, like Richard's had? What should I do? I wondered in panic. But I knew there was nothing I could do.

I eased the sheet on the jury-rigged sail, thought of taking it down, but knew with this wind I could make some headway, and every inch counted. I just hoped the jury rig would hold as it started to pour. It felt as if the spray and rain were drowning me, but *Hazana* was riding well, taking the seas on the starboard quarter. Was this the beginning of another hurricane? Without a radio I had no way of knowing what to expect. Fear rose in me as I faced the growing swells.

"SHOULD I GO BELOW? SHOULD I GO BELOW?" I cried out to The Voice.

Don't lose ground. Stay on course. Fight for your life, it ordered.

I leaped up and screamed at the clouds: "I'M NOT AFRAID OF YOU. YOU'RE NOTHING COMPARED TO HURRICANE RAYMOND. NOTHING. YOU'RE JUST A SQUALL. COME ON. COME ON, I'LL SHOW YOU. I'M ALIVE. ALIVE AND ALONE OUT HERE IN THE MIDDLE OF GOD KNOWS WHERE, SO COME ON, GET ME. I DARE YOU! COME AND GET ME! COME ON! TAKE ME TO RICHARD. I WANT RICHARD. RICHARD. I WANT RICH . . ."

I collapsed in the cockpit, wrapping my arms over my head to protect myself from the avalanche of rain and saltwater spray. I wept and finally begged.

"Please. Take me to Richard. I miss him so much. I can't stand this."

The driving rain on my back pounded the guilt deeper into my soul. I should not have left Richard alone topside. I should have stayed with him and torpedoed to oblivion. He had needed me and I had let him down. . . .

You didn't let him down, you helped him become a hero.

"I miss my hero. . . ."

As exhaustion dulled my guilt, I realized I should be collecting fresh water, but I just couldn't move. I leaned my head back and opened my mouth wide. The liquid I managed to swallow was salty. Perhaps I was now licking Mother Nature's tears.

The squall dispersed as quickly as it hit. I was spent yet cleansed, in a way. I hadn't realized how much I was still holding in. The storm had caused an explosion in the hollow hole in my heart that belonged to Richard. I had no control over it. I scared myself.

Times would be better, I told myself, when I reached latitude 19° N and could bear off to the left—port—and catch the trade winds for Hawaii. I sat and steered until late in the night, glad to be making headway toward my destination.

The next day I had newfound strength. Maybe I'd simply had enough of feeling sorry for myself. I decided to check out the fresh-water tank mounted under the cabin sole that connects to the sink. If I could get to an inspection plate I could unbolt, then I could lift it to see if any water was left in the tank. There was bound to be some. The first inspection plate I found was blocked by the floor framing. I searched through the scattered tools until I found a hammer and chisel, but the thought of chiseling through the wooden frame was daunting. Maybe there was another way. I grabbed a flashlight and started searching the top of the tank for another inspection plate.

Most of the tank was situated under the salon table and settee, making it hard to see, let alone reach. As I moved the beam of light around the fiberglass tank, I found another inspection plate, but it too was virtually impossible to get to without tearing the floor apart. Scanning the tank further, I found a loose wire with a connector on it dangling free. I moved the light across and saw the fitting on the tank. Excited, I extended my arm back into the narrow space, grabbed the loose wire, and stretched it back to where I could push the connector and fitting together. Getting up, I stepped over to the galley and tried the pressurized faucet at the sink. Nothing but sputtering and spitting. As I started to return to the tank, I saw that the water gauge on the galley bulkhead now read a quarter full. Apparently the fitting I had just reconnected was the gauge to measure the water level in the tank. I had a quarter of a tank of water! Overjoyed, I let the faucet sputter and spit air and then I filled a plastic cup to the top with the most delicious drink I had ever had in my life: cool, clear, sweet water. I filled the cup again. Oh, thank you, Lord, thank you. Mauruuru.

Encouraged, I went topside and danced around like Rocky, sharing with the world my life-saving find: "WATER, WATER, EVERYWHERE, AND ALL THE WHILE DID SNEAK; WATER, WATER, EVERYWHERE, NOW THERE'S LOTS TO DRINK!"

Prancing some more, I hollered, "YOU CAN'T KILL ME NOW. I'M GONNA LIVE, LIVE, LIVE. I HAVE WATER!" And with that I did every dance I had ever learned: the watusi, the jerk, the swim—winding down with a sexy bump and grind.

Laughing like a maniac, I hung onto the boom. Finding water was the most miraculous thing in the world to me. It left me giddy, even a bit hysterical. I had never been so thirsty as when I first realized I had to ration myself. Now, I no longer had to ration water, even though I would still have to be thrifty with the limited supply.

Discovering the water was a great turning point. I knew I would live, but more so, I felt as if I wanted to live. A tremendous weight had been lifted.

That night I danced with Richard on the deck. I looked up at one of our favorite constellations, Cassiopeia, the queen. She is the big *W* in the midst of the Milky Way.

"Isn't she wondrous?" Richard had always mused.

"Wondrous like you," I'd whisper in his ear, knowing he'd reply, "Wonderful like you."

"Richard . . ." I called as I slowly waltzed about the deck, "the W is for water, love. Did God and the heavens know? Was it fate? Why didn't we know? Wondrous, wonderful, water. Did Cassiopeia know water would take you from me? Did she approve, encourage it? Did she want you? Couldn't she have given us more time?" I put on Richard's shirt and hugged myself as I slowly danced. I closed my eyes. I didn't want to look at Cassiopeia anymore. I was jealous. Richard could be up there with her, waltzing along her wondrous path.

NINE

A Ship and a Gooseneck

Another long day. I tried to read a crinkly paperback thriller I had found in a cabinet while I munched on a can of cold kidney beans. I couldn't focus that long on the book's small print; soon my eyes were blurry, and my head ached.

Half asleep, trying to stay on course on the windless day, I saw, as if in a dream, a ship, a big ship, smoke curling from its stack, a foamy wake trailing behind. "A FOAMY WAKE!" I jumped up out of my daze. A ship? "A SHIP!" I yelled.

I grabbed the flare gun out of the waterproof bag I kept in the cockpit.

BAM! The noise startled me. The flare shot toward heaven, its brightness competing with the sun.

BAM! I fired the second flare.

I stared at the ship. Nothing. It didn't even alter course.

BAM! went the third flare.

The ship was getting smaller.

I grabbed a smoke bomb and lit it with the waterproof matches in the flare bag. I was so nervous that when it started to smoke I accidentally dropped it in the cockpit. I grabbed it to throw it overboard and burned my hand.

"Goddamn it!"

I grasped the oar with the red T-shirt tied onto it and rushed to the bow, frantically waving it as *Hazana* crested each swell. Nothing; the ship did not alter course one measly degree.

Throwing the oar down I hurried below to the VHF.

"Mayday! Mayday! Mayday! Do you read me? Over," I yelled into the microphone.

Nothing. Not one bloody burp.

"Mayday! Mayday! Mayday! Do you read me? Over." Nothing.

Dropping the mike, I hurried topside, grabbed the oar again, and waved. The ship diminished quickly over the horizon.

I was shocked. How could they not see me? I'm right here. What was I supposed to do—jump in and swim to the damn ship? I stomped around the deck, kicking whatever got in my way.

"They should have someone on watch. What kind of stupid ship is it, anyway? Idiots! You should be dry-docked," I screamed at the ship. "Moron. I hope your crew mutinies!"

"Aaaaaaaaaaaaaaaaaaaaah!" I screamed at the top of my

lungs and then in frustration stuck my hand in my mouth and bit it.

"OUCH."

Oh, that was smart, barked The Voice.

"JUST SHUT UP, SHUT UP. I HATE YOU AND THIS FUCKING BOAT. I HATE EVERYTHING IN THIS WHOLE GODDAMN, FUCKING, WET WORLD."

Even with that tirade spent, I was still full of rage. With adrenaline pumping through my veins I paced back and forth on the foredeck. I kicked the four-foot section of the mainmast still attached to the boom. It was driving me crazy to have to continually crawl under the broken mast or go around to the port side and climb over the life raft that was still attached to the side deck. The foot of the mainmast no longer benefited *Hazana,* but getting rid of it entailed the strenuous chore of removing the clevis pin holding it to the boom. I stood on the foredeck and shrieked at the severed mainmast: "AND YOU. I HATE YOU TOO. I CAN'T EVEN GET TO THE BOW WITH YOU THERE."

I found the hammer and a screwdriver in the mess of tools in the aft cabin. Sitting down on the deck, I beat on the stainless steel clevis pin. It didn't budge. I took out all my anger on that pin. Often I had to stop and rest. Finally, getting under the boom, I used my feet to lift the mast the fraction of an inch needed to relieve the pressure on the clevis pin. As the pin gave way, the foot of the mainmast, like a stump of a tree, toppled from the boom and fell on top of me, trapping me. Flat on my back near the edge of the deck I was terrified

Mainmast binnacle ripped from the deck

I'd fall overboard. As I tried to move, the jagged edges of the mainmast cut into my stomach. It weighed a ton. I didn't know what to do. I couldn't stay there; I had to get free. I lay gasping, staring at the sky, mustering every ounce of strength I could find to shove the massive piece of aluminum off me. As I lay there, I prayed, "Dear God, please help me. I'm sorry to be mad at you, I just don't understand all this. I'll try to be better. I'll . . . I'll—get this thing off me—one, two, three!" Arms pushed, feet shoved, stomach contracted, and every muscle in my body strained to break free. As the chunk of aluminum rolled off me, I caught myself along the toerail—the edge—just before the momentum could hurl me overboard.

I lay back against the warm deck, panting. How much more could I take? I should have realized the mast's foot would fall on me. What's the matter with me? My sanity was treading water.

As my breathing slowed, I closed my eyes and Richard's image came to me. "Hi, Sunshine," he said in his tender way.

I reached up and caressed his cheek. He smiled at me. I put my hand around his neck and pulled him down to me. As I started to kiss him, I kissed my own hand instead. My eyes flew open; the nightmare returned. I lay sobbing. Could he feel how much I missed him? Couldn't he just come to me for one minute, one lousy minute? Couldn't we be sitting inside *Mayaluga* again studying the charts at the nav station? Oh how I'd love to be making him a special meal again—the chicken enchiladas he loved so much, the meatless chili. I want to spend hours once more, cutting up fruit for sangria and vegetables for fresh salsa. I want to see his delight again, how he could eat like there was no tomorrow.

"Did you know, love, that there'd be no tomorrow?"

As I lay on the deck I was more shocked at the memory of thinking Richard was kissing me than I was at almost having been flung overboard. I gazed at the sky, the sun a full moon with a candlelit glow, and remembered how we'd aim at the full moon as we leaped off the bow pulpit. In flight I'd yell, "Fly me to the moon." In flight he'd dive and yell, "Fly me to the moon."

Richard had asked me, "Where should we go first?" when we were sitting in *Mayaluga*'s salon under the soft glow of the lantern's light. I should have said, "The moon," then he'd still be here. But he had said he wanted to go everywhere, and I had said, "Then everywhere we'll go." All the implications that I ever heard or read about, and all the images I had seen in movies of "real love" swam before my eyes. Richard was "Mr. Right," my knight in shining armor, my prince, my hero. He was confident and strong. He was opinionated and I liked that—I liked it that he knew what he wanted and would do whatever it took to get it. He wasn't afraid of physical labor—it was a means to an end for him. I liked that he trusted me and didn't fly off the handle when guys flirted with me. He knew I was at ease around men, having sailed and worked in boatyards. Their swearing or rough ways didn't throw me into a tizzy like it does a lot of women. Their demands didn't throw me off guard either. If someone suggested I do something I didn't want to do, I wouldn't, period. Richard liked that in me. He liked it that I was strong and capable too. I could be as feminine and sexy as the next woman if I wanted, but I preferred to be in the moment and if the moment required I be cranking on a winch to trim the jib, then by God, I'd crank until sweat rolled down my armpits and the job got done. If the moment became bathed in amore, then I could eagerly tack that way too. I like knowing that red is port and green is starboard, and red can mean stop and green can mean go. I like being a woman and being able to work like a man and I did like loving a man who could be as sensitive as a woman. I liked that a lot. . . .

The nights Richard and I lingered on *Mayaluga* at the dock in San Diego Bay were splendorous. We'd talked for hours and hours over where we'd go and what we'd do once winds. The north equatorial current runs between latitudes 10° N and 20° N. Because I had found my watch and could calculate my longitudinal position, I decided it would be better to stay in the lower portion of the eighteenth latitude until I got closer to Hawaii; then I could climb northwest through the latitudes toward my destination. This would also keep me in the path of more shipping lanes, where I hoped my flares would be seen.

As the night pushed away the day I made a pact with myself to try to stay awake longer into the night. My flares could be seen better at night if a ship were to appear.

Sitting under the star-filled sky I reflected on how different the night sky is in the northern and southern latitudes. I thought I could see the Southern Cross, but it was just a memory floating in my mind. It would be a long night, so I lay back and let my mind float.

"Remember our floating contests, Richard? How we'd challenge each other? Being so lean, you could float as easily as a seal."

"You have to be able to float for an hour, Tami," you used to tell me—"For a whole bloody hour, love."

I thought you were nuts—"An hour! Nobody floats for an hour," I protested. Remember that? And you said, "A sailor can float for an hour." So then I did it. Then we did it together, a whole hour floating around each other with heads touching and with feet touching, back-paddling to stay together. A whole hour, love ... I wish I had that hour back. I wish we could do it again. I wish we could be

we got there. Richard loved how excited I became describing the islands and atolls. I pointed out places I'd heard of and yet somehow had missed. He promised me we'd go there. I described how different French Polynesian society is from ours—slow and calm—and I elaborated on how the cultures of the islands and atolls are each so different in their own way.

He confessed that he wanted to experience it all. "I can't wait to go, love," he said, "to take you there again."

Putting my arms around his neck and drawing his face close to mine I pledged, "I'll go anywhere with you, Richard, anywhere."

That's when I kissed him and started to sing "Fly Me to the Moon," and we laughed and laughed, then jumped up, peeled off our clothes, and aimed for the moon as we dived into the sea off the bow.

TEN

La Cascade

After the horror of almost falling off *Hazana*, I decided to trail a three-quarter-inch rope off the stern in case I fell in. Even with *Hazana* traveling only one or two knots, I knew I might not have the strength to swim fast enough to catch up with her. If I did fall in I could at least attempt to grab onto the rope. It terrified me to think I could possibly drown after all these lonely and miserable days of struggling to survive.

Looking behind me, I could see the rope leaving the stern, but I couldn't see it tracking underwater. Nevertheless, it gave me a great sense of security to know it streamed about twenty-five feet behind *Hazana*.

Most days were about the same, sailing along at a snail's pace, but I did see progress each time I noted my LOP on the chart, plus if I kept rationing I should have enough water and food to survive.

Sardines were my favorite meal. The flat, oval container was so distinctive that there was no mistaking the contents, even with the label washed off. I knew I shouldn't eat them— their salt content was way too high, making me thirsty after each delicious bite—but sometimes I just didn't care. I craved them. I'd hold out and hold out, and then finally when I couldn't take it anymore, I'd snap the can opener onto the rim, watch the oil ooze out, then crank the delicacy open. Using my fingers, I'd dig in, grabbing a small slimy fish by its tail, and then nibble away. I'd spend an hour savoring half a can, saving the other half for later.

I stayed on a starboard tack, crawling to latitude 19° N. I was beginning to get apprehensive about seeking the higher latitude because the winds seemed to be getting fluky. There is sixty miles between each latitude, which gives the wind sixty miles to diminish or become unpredictable, or even to piddle-out dead calm. The wind had been steadier in the lower 18° N latitude.

I went down to the nav station and grabbed a couple of cruising guides that hadn't been ruined in the capsize and brought them topside. I wanted to study the books in hope they would help me analyze my situation.

I decided to use the north equatorial current as much as I could to push me west. The current's force against the hull helped drag *Hazana* through the water, and I could make better time by using the current than by using the unsteady in Fatu Hiva hiking up to La Cascade and floating once more.

<hr>

We knew La Cascade would be far, but not as far as it turned out to be. We hiked for another hour. The trail was rocky and treacherous, with switchbacks that led up the side of the mountain, but finally leveled out and headed west to the sea. The path became narrow and fell two hundred feet down to the surf pounding the rocks below. I couldn't look down. It made me dizzy. The trail had virtually disintegrated in this spot. Richard went first. I stood by, quietly saying a little prayer. There was only enough room for one foot to rest on the tiny ledge. Holding onto the rock outcropping with his left hand, Richard moved his left foot onto the ledge. His foot slipped, causing volcanic rock and dust to tumble into the surf below. I sucked in my breath. Richard's grip on the crevasse and his right foot kept him grounded. With the heel of his left shoe he kicked at the narrow ledge, making a better foothold. "Not to worry, love," he casually said to me. I watched him gauge his momentum and then swing his right leg around the sharp ridge, landing on solid ground. "Nothing to it." He beamed at me.

"I don't know about this," I murmured, not looking him in the eye.

"As you swing around, stretch out your hand, and I'll grab your wrist. I promise."

"I don't know. . . ."

"Come on, love. We can't have come this bloody far to give up now."

"I hate heights," I whined.

"You go up the mast."

"That's different; I have safety lines holding me when I'm up there."

"It's not as bad as it looks," he said encouragingly.

"Okay, okay. Just be ready."

"I will, I promise."

I followed his foot pattern, and as I swung around he grabbed my wrist and pulled me over to land. "Th-that wasn't so bad," I stuttered.

"That's my girl," he said with a huge smile.

We continued over the trail, which had started to climb, and we took more breaks as we got winded. My calves and thighs ached. As I turned my gaze in the direction of La Cascade, I was dumbfounded. The massive waterfall hissed and roared as it plunged into the reservoir, creating swirling pools of cloudy blue. Sparkling vapor rose and clung to the foliage, collecting dew and dripping it back, reborn, into the natural pool. Pandanus, mimosa, paper mulberry, aito, haari, and nui trees covered with bromeliads rustled in the wind from the force of the falls. The fragrant frangipani, passion flowers, and birds of paradise blazed in the jungle and scented the air. Philodendron leaves were like hands waving in the great waterfall's breeze. Never had I seen such a mesmerizing sight.

In the calm area of the pond in front of us, something undulated. Could it be an underwater eddy? I wondered. A large flat rock in the middle of the pool basked in the sun.

We jumped down off the boulder and Richard took me by the hand as we walked around the perimeter of the pool to a level grassy area. A perfect picnic site. Looking at the water I saw the undulation again. "Richard—eels," I squealed and turned in time to see him in the midst of a perfect dive into the crisp cobalt blue water. His pack and shorts lay piled up on the water's edge. The eels' shimmery skin glistened in the sunshine. The idea of eels slinking against my body, scooting around my legs, nibbling on a toe . . . yuck.

Richard surfaced with a loud Tarzan cry, pounding his muscular bronzed chest. "Come on in, love, the water's great."

"Richard, there's eels!"

"No big deal, love. They're more afraid of you than you are of them. Trust me, come on. . . ."

"No way." I set my backpack down, getting out my towel.

Richard swam all over the pond, splashing and whooping it up. I sat on my towel in the sun and watched the water cascade off the high cliff.

Soon sweat was rolling down my armpits and cleavage. It was sweltering. The eels didn't seem to be bothering Richard. What the hell, I mumbled to myself. I pulled off my pareu, curled up like a cannon ball, and jumped in.

The water felt cool, refreshing as it washed over my sun-burned body. The water was so clean, thin—not dense like the salty sea. I surfaced, taking a deep breath. A feeling of rejuvenation surged through me. I swam around stretching my arms out wide, freely kicking my legs. Floating without a care in the world, I stared up at the sky framed by the lush foliage surrounding us. Ah, if this wasn't heaven, I didn't know what could be. Richard floating too, floated up next to me. There we drifted, my feet one way, his the other, striving to stay cheek to cheek.

"Come on, let's explore," he finally suggested. We treaded through the water to get as close to the waterfall's intense shower as we could. Taking deep breaths we dove under the waterfall, where I tried to open my eyes but couldn't. We both surfaced, gasping for air.

"Look over here," said Richard as he guided me away from the mainstream of the falls to the smaller side falls. "Let's sit here for a minute and let the falling water massage us." We lounged under the descending water and let its fingers knead our hardened bodies. As my muscles relaxed, I heard Richard's voice echo out from behind one of the gentler falls. "You should see this, love." I waded over to him behind the pewter curtain. He pulled me onto his lap and he kissed my palms, my shoulders, my neck. Our bodies united, our souls became one. We made love matching the intensity of the cascading waterfall. We stayed in each other's arms for a long time while our pounding hearts quieted. Richard's stomach suddenly growled. We started laughing.

"Hungry, love?" I teased.

"I guess."

"Then I have a feast for you, my wild man. Take me to shore, and I'll serve you."

Richard scooped me up in his arms and plowed through the curtain of water. "I am a caveman bringing my woman home. You belong to me; you're mine, all mine." And he howled like Tarzan again to the jungle.

"How did I get so lucky?" I pecked his lips and then pushed against his shoulders. He let me slip into the water.

"Last one to the food's a rotten egg!" I blurted out. Pushing off with my feet I swam like crazy toward the shore of our grassy beach. I hit my towel, panting. Richard grabbed me, I giggled, and he gave me a monstrous kiss. "God, how I love you," he whispered in my ear.

I laid out our feast: French bread, cheese, canned liver pâté, and papaya. "The beer's in the shade under that pandanus tree," I said, pointing to a spot in the water a few feet away. We sat in comfortable silence and ate, taking in all the divine wonder around us. I thought again, surer this time, this had to be heaven.

Feeling sleepy, we moved our towels over to a shady spot. I snuggled my back into the curve of Richard's body and fell asleep. The next thing I knew he was nibbling on my ear, whispering, "Sorry, love. It's time to go."

Packing our belongings, we left the last of the bread for the black noddy birds watching us from the trees. "I will never forget this place," I said, taking one last look as we headed out.

"Nor will I, love, nor will I."

Back at the village we rowed out to *Mayaluga* as the sun set. The water looked like pounded copper. The warm breeze ruffled the palm leaves, playing peekaboo with the night's first stars. We saw a fire up the beach and watched some locals gathering wood.

"See how proudly Leo sits in the sky?" Richard asked.

"Which constellation is Leo?" I yawned, teasing him.

"Right below the Big Dipper; he curves like a backward question mark. I feel like Leo tonight."

"King of the jungle, or a backward question mark?"

Laughing, he said, "Definitely king of the jungle."

"Just look at that magnificent sky," he continued. "It's a great big canvas of light. One constellation enhancing another, full of mythological stories. What stands out most to you?"

"The Southern Cross."

"Exactly. But, what does that simple cross up there mean to you?" he asked.

"I never really gave it much thought. I just know when I see it up there I'm in the southern hemisphere. What does it mean to you?"

"It means I have traveled a long way from the different constellations of my childhood sky in England. It gives me enlightenment. See the direction the staff points?"

"Yes."

"It points to the south celestial pole. Too bad there's not a 'South Star' like there's a North Star." Richard sighed deeply. "I do feel blessed with Crux up there shining down on us, but I feel more blessed with you here beside me. It's fate, Tami. I sailed half the world to find you."

Richard stretched his left hand out to me. I grasped it. It was warm and strong. I looked up at his angular profile and noticed the glint of a tear in his eye. I wanted to squeeze his hand, to bring that gaze of love back to me, but I realized I had caught an unguarded glimpse of my lover's soul. He had returned his gaze to the sky and the privacy of his thoughts. It was not for me to invade.

Our hands stayed grasped together in the center of the cockpit. I, too, returned to the theater in the sky, remembering something my mom used to say: "God's in his heaven; all's right with the world."

I felt this night would stay with me forever.

Richard held his right hand up to the moon. "The old man's waxing," he said.

"How can you tell?" I questioned.

"See how my right hand caresses the right side, the full side, of the moon?"

I let go of his left hand and held my right hand up to caress the moon. "Yes."

"That means he's waxing, getting full. If your left hand could circle the full side of the moon, that would mean he's waning."

"I don't know about this."

"It's true. I learned it from an old salt in South Africa. By the look of this moon it should be full in less than a week. If we want to arrive in the Tuamotus on a full moon, we should probably leave here soon."

ELEVEN

Hinanos and Cigars

It was hard for me to look at the moon and care whether it was waning or waxing. If I hit land on a moonless and starless night I could care less. I just wished my landfall would be tomorrow. I was so tired of looking at nothing beyond the carpet of ocean and the curtain of sky.

My day-to-day schedule had come to focus entirely around my three daily sun sights. At night, if I had good wind, I'd steer *Hazana* as long as I could stay awake. Then I'd lash the wheel and sleep in the cockpit until the morning sun forced me, sweating profusely, from my sleeping bag.

My first chore upon rising was to look three hundred sixty degrees around the horizon. Nothing was there, ever, but water and sky.

My second chore took me forward to check the jury rig, to see if any lines were chafing. I made sure the luff of the sail was tight. The rig had become my companion, always there, pulling the boat inch by inch toward the solid ground I longed for.

If there was no wind, I'd lash the wheel and force myself to go below. I made notes in the logbook like, "Paranoia! Becalmed. Still in the same spot as yesterday. God, I miss Richard. When is this streak of the devil going to end?"

I didn't want to think of the devil—Satan. This was enough hell for me. But my imagination started taking over. I warily looked around and started shaking. I hugged myself, trying to stop the involuntary rattle. The devil was here, near, coming to get me. . . .

You're making your own hell, exploded The Voice.

"I didn't make this!"

Control your mind—you're your own heaven and hell! Think positive. Move. Take care of yourself.

I wanted to plug my ears, but I liked what The Voice had to say better than what my mind said in thought. I went to wipe sweat from my brow and winced as the salt on my hand singed the wound on my forehead. It ignited me. I stood up and went into the head to clean and dress my wounds. I didn't like this job, but when the bandage became grimy and unsanitary, I had no choice; I was terrified of infection.

Down below, debris still littered the bilge. The floorboards were thrown about the cabin. I found it easier to move around by stepping on the floor framing and parts of the bilge than to try to figure out which floorboard went where. The scattered beans were sprouting and the oatmeal grew moldier by the day. Occasionally, a rusted can burst and started to stink, then I'd toss it overboard. It was simply easier on my nostrils and nerves to stay topside.

Finally, the gnawing reality of living in a pigsty became too much. I couldn't take the filth and stench anymore. The Voice interceded: *It's disgusting in here.*

"I know it."

You need to continue the cleanup.

"I don't feel like it; it makes me sick."

It would make you less sick if you'd clean it up.

"You clean it up."

It's your job.

"I'm in charge here—it's not my job!" I said cockily.

I stood a moment trying to decide who should win, The Voice or me.

Ultimately I realized it was a no-win situation. I scooped up buckets of saltwater and started scrubbing. When I got tired of that, I started picking up cans of food and stockpiling them in the galley. Broken glass made me angry all over again. We should not have left so much glass on board.

As I cleaned, I found having to continually step over the rolled-up, deflated orange dinghy a pain in the neck. Even though it weighed a ton, I was on a mission. I dragged and pulled it across the cabin, then catapulted it into the cockpit. Once topside, I rolled it aft and lashed it to the stern rail on the port aft-quarter.

Going back below, I discovered three plastic bottles of

hand and body lotion. This must be good stuff, I thought, for the owner, Christine, to have stored so many. Christine was a pretty woman. Ah, to feel pretty again.

I went to the mirror in the head and stared at myself. Even though tan, I looked pale. There were bags under my eyes, I was drawn, and my mouth had a perpetual pout. The bandage on my forehead was smudged with dirt and the paisley print bandanna crowned everything. What was I, I wondered, the Queen of Doom? I flipped the cap open and smelled the lotion. It smelled wonderful, the fragrance fresh and clean, citrus with a hint of floral. I squirted some in the palm of my hand, and then rubbed it on my cheek. It felt cold, soothing. I rubbed my other cheek, then my eyelids, nose, and chin. I stayed away from my wounded forehead.

I tried to smile at the mirror's reflection, but my lips were dry, cracked. I rubbed them hard with the lotion, trying to smooth away the crevices, but it didn't help much. I looked so weird, I scared myself. I didn't want to acknowledge the fears under the surface of the person I was looking at. It was a balancing act: I realized if I wavered too far I would go off the deep end.

I turned away from the sorry image in the mirror and made my way to the settee in the main salon, where I sat down and proceeded to make trails of lotion along both arms. The cool sensation briefly raised goose bumps, but the satiny cream fed them and they disappeared as quickly as they rose. My skin sucked in the lotion. I spent a long time giving every pore on my body a taste. Between my toes, back of my neck, even my armpits. I couldn't get enough. When I finished I realized I had nearly emptied the container.

Snapping the cap of the lotion shut, I looked around the cabin and thought, why even bother with this mess?

Because it still stinks, remember? You haven't finished cleaning.

With a deep sigh, I picked up my foul-weather pants to hang in the locker. Jammed cockeyed was a heavy metal object wrapped in a towel. I unswirled the tip of the towel to find the barrel of a rifle.

"No—no, no, no," I said, and roughly pushed it back, cramming the pants inside and slamming the locker shut.

I lowered myself to my knees and started cleaning a settee locker. Reaching deep under the seat I felt something cold and pulled my hand away quickly. Grabbing the flashlight I shined it back toward the corner. Metal tins. I reached in and slid the containers out. Cigars! What on earth were cigars doing on board? I hadn't noticed Peter, the owner of *Hazana*, smoking them. Maybe they were for trading. I tore off the seal and lifted the lid of the tin. The aroma actually cheered me. In the past, cigarettes and cigars had disgusted me, but today they felt like a touch of humanity. The scent gave me a sense of being in the real world.

I dug deeper into the settee and pulled out a big tin of Arnott's biscuits. "Ummm." I surprised myself. My appetite must be returning. I tore off the lid and ate one, savoring each crunchy bite.

"What else is hiding in this gold mine?" Turning sideways, I reached way in. My fingertips scraped a cardboard box.

Stretching with all my might my fingers hooked and dragged the heavy box to the opening of the settee. Ripping it open, I discovered a case of Hinano beer—Richard's and my favorite.

"Man, I could get wasted on this," I announced to no one. "I bet if I drank it all, I could die of alcohol poisoning."

What would be the point?

"The point would be to quit remembering the good times I will never have again."

Do you wish you had never had those good times?

"I wouldn't give them up for anything."

Then enjoy remembering them.

Sometimes I hated The Voice. It slapped me with logic every chance it got. No sympathy for my plight. Grabbing a bottle of beer, a cigar, the bottle opener, and some waterproof matches from the galley, I went topside. There was no wind; the sun was setting. Straddling the boom, I bit the end off the cigar just as I'd seen in movies and spit it overboard. I stuck the cigar in my mouth, biting it with my front teeth, and struck a match to its tip. Sucking and coughing, I finally got the stogie lit. I snapped the bottle cap off the Hinano and watched it sail through the air. Even though the beer was warm, it tasted like nectar. Feeling like King Tut on his throne, I lounged there, contemplating the passing of another day.

Could that bright star near the horizon, the one with the red hue, be Fomalhaut, the eye of Piscis Austrinus, the Southern Fish? I knew Fomalhaut was one of the four royal stars of ancient astrology. I could see no other bright stars near it—

must be Fomalhaut. Later, I would look for the water carrier, Aquarius, and find the jar he carries and spills down onto the Southern Fish. As the last bit of light seeped from the sky, the winged horse, Pegasus, galloped into view—Pegasus from the blood of snaked-haired Medusa. As the myth goes, Perseus killed Medusa in one of his heroic deeds. Studying the sky further, I found Grus, the crane, and Lacerta, the lizard. If I looked hard enough, would I find Richard, the missing man? I pictured Richard's gentle face inside the great square of Pegasus. If only we could be straddling the boom together, smoking cigars and drinking warm Hinano beer. If only . . .

I heard the foot of the sail scrape taut along the port side of the deck. Ah, some wind. I finished my beer and stubbed out my cigar, then climbed down from the boom, unlashed the wheel, and started steering. At least at night I had the stars to entertain me and the moon to get lost in.

TWELVE

Machetes and Eels

Some time before dawn, a cloud in the shape of a maple leaf fanned the slivered moon. I strained my eyes, but I was still at sea, *Hazana* was still mastless, and Richard was still gone.

Coming topside from calculating my morning sight, I found a booby bird sitting on top of the jury-rigged mast. Booby birds have been known to follow ships for days—perching in their rigging, so seeing it wasn't that big of a surprise. The bird was about thirty inches tall and mainly white. I was fascinated with its beady eyes and powder blue eye shadow. The feathers around its beak were also a pretty blue hue. For an instant the bird's eyes opened wider, becoming Richard's. The powder blue coalesced into that lapis color of Richard's eyes, the color that could melt me with one long look. But as the bird wiggled, its huge pumpkin orange webbed feet broke the spell and once again it was only a bird come to haunt me. The bird left, but a couple of hours later it returned to use the rig again for its resting post. It squawked and slept a lot, and then, after preening itself, flew away to fish once more. The booby stayed with me for three days, but when its droppings started to stink, I tried to shoo it away with the red T-shirt–covered oar. The damn bird kept coming back again and again, and I kept chasing it, apologizing and saying if it wouldn't poop it could stay. Finally it had had enough of me and flew away for good. Then I missed staring into those blue eyes and the sign of life on board.

October 31. Halloween. Nineteen days since the capsize. With a steady wind, I had traversed forty miles in the past twenty-four hours, according to the noon fix. I thought about all my Halloweens as a kid, the getting dressed up, the trick or treating with my friends. I remembered the year I got so sick. I was seven years old, and my grandparents had rented a flapper costume for me. I loved it because the fringe sewn on the satin material shimmied and the beaded head band glowed with fake gemstones. At the third house, I became ill. I was devastated to have to go home: my bag of candy had only three pieces in it, and no one else would get to see me in my wonderful costume. I wondered what my three-year-old half brother would be this year, probably a pirate or a cowboy.

Eating meant very little to me. But that night on *Hazana*, I decided to make myself a treat to take the edge off this trick I was living in. I opened a small canned ham and poured half a jar of plum sauce over it. The plum sauce was such a treat, especially since the jar hadn't broken, that I wouldn't allow myself to eat it all in one meal. I relished it with peanut butter and crackers. For dessert I delighted over bites of canned pears. Eating all that food at once made me sick, but I couldn't stop.

You better stop. You need to ration your food, there's only one duffel bag of canned goods left.

"Good, maybe I'll end up starving to death."

Not if you keep eating the way you just ate.

"Hey, it's Halloween and that was my treat. What's your treat, Voice, or do you have a trick up your invisible sleeve?"

You, Tami. You are my treat.

"Huh, some treat . . ."

November 1, I lackadaisically scanned the sea with the binoculars as I did thirty to a hundred times a day. Suddenly I spotted something orange on the horizon. It was a large tangerine buoy with a red flag tied alongside it. I could see the bright buoy only as it crested the swells.

"Wow, will you look at that," I said to the cleat that held Richard's empty tether.

I altered course and about an hour later got close enough to the buoy to see that there was a net attached to it. Should I tie up to the net and wait for the fishing boat to return? What if it never returned? I wasn't sure what to do.

As I collected myself and studied the net again, I realized it must have been abandoned. It was too covered with barnacles and fouled with streeling seaweed to have been set recently. No one was coming back for this net. I should sail on. I had already wasted two hours of precious time.

I sailed an amazing sixty miles the next day, and fifty the day after that. I was obviously in the north equatorial current and making good time. I was pleased I had listened to my intuition and returned to the lower 18° N latitudes. I estimated only 590 miles to go to reach Hawaii. Only! Here I'd crawled at a snail's pace over a thousand miles of the Pacific Ocean all alone, and I was thinking "only." Land was near, yet still so very, very far.

"I wish my skipper were here," I wrote in the logbook.

For the next two days it was rainy and the seas were rough.

The sun's rays penetrated my eyelids, causing a white light so bright it woke me. I got up, unlashed the wheel, and began to steer. The sail billowed out, full of wind. The seas had calmed and *Hazana* was making much better time. She pushed through the water, making at least two knots. It felt exhilarating as I sat propped up by some pillows against the cockpit coaming. I liked steering with my foot, my toes wrapped around a cool stainless steel spoke. My mind buzzed with alertness after hours of sleep. So, as always, I'd think. I'd think and think and think.

I wondered, why is there life anyway? How are earth, water, sky, stars, people, animals all connected? Are we connected? I had felt connected to Minka, the German shepherd I had growing up. She could read my mind: She always knew when I was sad or melancholy, not quite up to par. I wished she was sitting beside me, her soft, furry head in my lap. I remembered how often Richard and I would have the same thought, a mental telepathy. Could he and I still think the same things? Could he feel how much I miss him? If only Richard could be pointing toward land again and we both could shout at once, "There's the entrance!" It seemed like we always said the same things at once.

"There's the entrance!" Richard and I both shouted. We were excited about visiting the Tuamotu Archipelago—the largest group of atolls in the world.

Sailing directions warned boaters that the current could rip through the sixty-foot-wide entrance to Raroia at eight knots. We waited for the end of the tide's ebb; it was just about slack before we ventured into the cut and anchored in a sandy bottom in front of a small village. While we were stowing gear from our four-day journey, a twenty-foot runabout motored out to us. The driver skillfully pulled up next to *Mayaluga* and turned off his engine. He introduced himself as Remy and invited us to come and share lunch with his family.

On shore, we walked with Remy up to his small house, where his family greeted us. He introduced his wife, Lucy, their daughter, Sylvia, and Sylvia's fiancé, Kimo. We were made comfortable outside in chairs on the sand, enjoying the smell of fresh tuna being barbecued.

Suddenly I noticed a black-tipped dorsal fin out in the

lagoon. As I sat up and stared, both Richard and I said at once, "Sharks!"

Remy laughed and shrugged his shoulders. He then spoke rapidly to Richard, who explained to me that the locals leave the reef sharks alone, as they are only curious about people and not eager to bite them. But Remy suggested that we keep a dinghy nearby us while swimming in the lagoon to leap into should the sharks get too close.

Remy mentioned that they didn't work harvesting copra—dried coconut—on Sundays, and that they would love to show us Kon Tiki Island, across the lagoon.

We took off the next day towing their runabout behind *Mayaluga* and arrived at Kon Tiki Island in the early afternoon. Richard and I felt in awe of being at the sandy islet where the famous balsa raft *Kon-Tiki* had run aground in 1947 after sailing from Peru in one hundred and one days.

We pulled Remy's runabout up to *Mayaluga* and the family of four climbed into it and took off for shore. We lowered our dinghy into the water and soon followed behind. They were bustling about setting up camp when we hauled our dinghy up onto the beach. Kimo started walking up the beach, then turned and waved for Richard to follow—he was going fishing.

Sylvia and I went looking for shells. Digging through the grains of coral I discovered a beautiful spiked shell the size of my fist. I became so intent on my unusual gem that I fell backward in surprise when I glanced up and saw black, beady eyes staring at me. Two black-tipped sharks were only two feet away from me. Taking a deep breath, I realized they weren't going to leap out of the water and eat me, but it was unnerving to know they could so silently intrude. They did appear to be only curious, but I decided not to shell so close to the water after that!

The next morning we took a long walk. The tide action felt good on my ankles, and I tended to lag behind, forever the sheller. All of a sudden, there was a frenzy of splashing in front of me and in an instant of fluid motion, Lucy swung her machete around and whacked the head off a moray eel.

"My God," I said, stunned. Lucy continued on, unfazed. I watched the body of the eel squirm and twist to its death. Now I knew why they always carried machetes. I stopped shelling and hung close to Lucy's side. I felt a new respect for her. Perhaps Lucy had mental telepathy too.

THIRTEEN

Overboard

My foot slipped off *Hazana*'s wheel and hit the cockpit sole with a loud thud. I had been concentrating, trying to send a mental message to Richard. Perhaps the thud was his way of giving me a kick in the butt, reminding me to pay attention and stay on course.

You think too much, The Voice gently said, startling me.

"What else is there to do? I'm trying to mentally send Richard a message."

What do you want to tell him?

"That I would live through all this again, just to have him back in my life once more."

He wants you to know he would too. . . .

Lifting my foot back up on the spoke and giving a little push to port, I thought of Richard going overboard and what a waste it was of human life. The Voice interrupted my thoughts: *The only waste is your feeling sorry for yourself. You have no right to judge that Richard's life was a waste. You are not God.*

I felt ashamed, but then became defensive: "Hey, Voice, no problem, I'll never fall in love again."

Now, that would be a waste.

I smiled at The Voice's wit and turned the wheel. I noticed a stiff jerkiness in the helm's action. It had happened before, on and off. I knew I could not keep ignoring the fact that something might be damaged or fouled on the rudder under the boat. It made steering a challenge, in that it was like an isometric exercise, tiring my arms, to keep on course. I had inspected the wheel and steering cable topside a couple of times, but nothing seemed askew. I knew I had to check the rudder, and the only way to do that was by jumping in the water, diving under the boat, and taking a look. The thought scared me. Who would pull me back on board if something went wrong? What if a shark attacked me? I didn't want to think about it anymore. I'd deal with it later.

The sky twinkled an unreadable Morse code. The stars were sending messages of encouragement my way. A shooting star meant I could have a wish. My wishes were always the same: Let Richard be alive; someone please find me; give me the courage to dive under the boat. I loved this time of day, the edge of dawn. It seemed magical to watch the stars go to sleep one by one as the sun woke up.

This day, the sunrise painted the sky with Maxfield Parrish hues. I could feel serenity. Was God serenity? I lashed the wheel and went to the bow.

Unwrapping my flowered pareu, I let it slip to the deck, where I sat down on it, cross-legged, nude. I rested my arms on my legs, palms up, ready to receive all the good vibrations the universe would give me. Rays of pastel colors permeated my hair, my eyes, my skin, my forearms, my legs, my air, and my soul. I took in a deep, cleansing breath through my nostrils, more air and more air, then let it out through my mouth with a *whooo*. I could feel the marrow in my bones warming in the morning's placid heat. I melted into harmony with all that was around me. At least for this brief time, I loathed nothing nor longed for anything. I felt no fear and experienced no pain. The bliss of the pastel morning had its own melodious song, its own gospel, its own amazing grace.

My meditation gave me strength. Optimism engulfed me, and I found myself struck with the knowledge that what is meant to be—is. Richard's time was up. There was maybe one chance in a million he could still be alive. Even if he had come below with me he might still have died. Wouldn't that have been worse? Not quick, like the power of the monstrous wave that must have knocked the last breath out of him.

I contemplated what makes it a person's time. Does God decide? Do our actions on earth decide? I'd been a good person. I didn't consciously try to hurt people. I didn't lie or steal. I believed I needed to treat people the way I wanted to be treated. We are all equal, no exceptions. But Richard was a good person, too. So, why was I still alive? Why wasn't it my time also? What was I living for? What would I do now with the rest of my life?

The tears that rolled down my face and dripped onto my breasts were cleansing tears. They were mourning tears and healing tears, cascading into one. The questions I asked myself were therapeutic. I was achingly accepting my circumstances and slowly starting to mend.

I was sure the Bible said something about many mansions in the Father's house. Does that mean we live again? I wondered. To me it did. I wanted Richard to be reborn, to live again. I wanted to know him again, to talk to him again, to love him again. And maybe that's why I was meant to live, so I'd get to know and love him in a different way the next time. All I could do would be to live on and find out. Someday it would be my time, but not yet, and that was the hardest guilt to get over.

With a deep breath, in and out, I opened my eyes and peered into the light of the sun. Its intensity blinded me, humbled me. Once again, I bowed my head to the great Creator and simply said, "Protect me, God, your sea is so big and this boat is so small. Amen."

Opening my eyes I peered into the deep turquoise sea. It appeared calm, gentle. It beckoned me. Yes, I could dive under the boat today. With renewed energy and faith, I got up and stretched, lowered the sail to the deck so *Hazana* would drift, and grabbed my cheerful pareu as I went aft to the cockpit. I dug around in the seat lockers and found two ropes and my dive mask. Should I eat first?

No, dive first; then give yourself a treat.

"Fruit cocktail?"

Ummm, yes. It sounds delicious.

I took off my bandanna and laid it on the seat locker. I briefly touched my hair—no—I did not need to think about my matted hair. It would only force me backward. Start with diving under the boat, I told myself.

I grabbed the two ropes and tied them onto the winch with a couple of half hitches. Then I tied each rope around my waist with a bowline knot. I still had the three-quarter-inch line trailing in the water off the stern.

As I stood on the side of the deck, I asked God to protect me. Then I took a deep breath and jumped in feet first. The water felt chilly but surprisingly refreshing. The saltwater burned my cuts, my head especially, but I didn't mind—it was healing. I couldn't remember the last decent shower I had taken. Since the capsize, I had either poured a bucket of saltwater over me or wiped myself down with a washcloth dampened sparsely with fresh water, but now, being totally submerged in the saltwater, every pore on my body was cleansed. I treaded water, allowing myself to get acclimated, and then put my mask on. I tried not to think about this being the same cruel water that had taken Richard from me. I took a deep breath and dove under the boat. The water was clear and refreshing. Seven four- to five-foot mahi-mahis hovered against the hull. The bottom of the boat looked ominous with its large keel and small rudder. I surfaced for another breath as I tried to keep my anxiety and fear at bay.

Diving deeper, I swam toward the propeller. I could see that one of the mizzen shrouds had wrapped itself around the propeller's shaft. After going up for air again, I dove back under and tried pulling on the shroud, but it had welded itself onto the shaft. It would just have to trail along. I hated that it would cause drag through the water, impeding *Hazana*'s progress, but there was nothing I could do. There was no way I could hold my breath long enough to try to cut the shroud free, nor would I have the strength. Surfacing, I grabbed another mouthful of air and plunged down to survey the rudder. I turned it side to side and inspected it for any damage or obstructions. It seemed to be working fine, which added to the mystery of why the steering was stiff. With nothing more to check under the water I surfaced, took hold of a rope, pulled myself up to the stern and made my way up the ladder. Winded, I shook my head in disappointment, remembering how strong I used to be. Oh well, stiff steering is better than no steering. I was just thankful the rudder was in its place so I could steer at all. Feeling proud of myself for jumping in the water and overcoming my fear, I finished patting dry and went to the bow and set the sail. After digging through the duffel bag for a can of fruit cocktail, I sat in the cockpit steering, delighting in each bite. Every time I came to a halved red cherry, I set it aside, creating a small mountain of crimson sugar to devour in one great big bite.

May I have one? The Voice meekly asked.

I stared at my growing mound of cherries and thought, what the hell. "Sure—help yourself," I said, then chuckled, because it was The Voice that needed my help for a change. This felt good.

FOURTEEN

Turtle Back Sunsets

I took off my hat and lifted my face to the sun. A shadow crossed over my closed eyelids. Shading my eyes from the glare, I looked up at the sky. A pair of frigate birds were soaring in the wind. This was Day Twenty-six after the capsize. I had just taken my noon sight and calculated 480 miles to go. Seeing the birds felt like a good sign to me—land must be near. I gazed up in awe, admiring the frigates' seven-foot wingspans and their deeply forked tails. I watched them tuck their giant wings against their bodies and dive as fast as bullets toward the sea. At the last minute they'd pluck an unsuspecting fish from just below the surface of the water as they ricocheted back up into the sky. I knew that these birds could spend days out at sea, soaring on thermal drafts. They never land on water, because their short legs and long wings make it difficult, if not impossible, to take off.

I couldn't bring myself to catch fish to eat. I would have to kill them. Death had taken on a new meaning for me now. Canned sardines were just fine. They were already dead, the life knocked out of them.

I spent many hours watching the frigates. Sometimes I'd follow their motions with the binoculars. It made me dizzy. The female was more aggressive, easily stealing food from the male. I decided he let her have it, for they must be lovers; he wanted to share.

When a different bird flew into view, I sat up and grabbed *Hazana*'s binoculars. It was a tropicbird, about the size of a gull only with a long, white, tapering tail. It was primarily white with an orange beak, black eye shadow, and black tips to its wings. It would have nothing to do with the frigates— most birds won't, because the frigates are so big and mean. All these birds were a definite sign I must be approaching Hawaii.

I dug out my next to last can of sardines and my second to last bottle of beer. I was sick of cold chili, cold beans, and cold canned vegetables. I loved sardines. If the birds could eat what they loved, why couldn't I?

Five days passed uneventfully. I established a routine of waking up sometime between three and six in the morning, depending on the wind and swells. I'd check the rig, meditate on the bow, open a can, and eat whatever was in it. It was always a surprise, since the labels had fallen off most of the canned goods. I'd try to pick a can I thought was fruit for breakfast. Then I'd scan the horizon with the binoculars, and sit and steer for hours and hours. I still couldn't read. I couldn't concentrate on words.

Noon was the most exciting time of day, because I would take my second sun sight and calculate how far I had traveled in the past twenty-four hours. It was always somewhere between twenty and sixty nautical miles. I just prayed I would hit one of the Hawaiian Islands and not sail past them. It didn't have to be the big island of Hawaii I came to, even though that would be the closest. Any island would do.

I constantly thought about my past with Richard and what my future would be now that he was gone. My grandpa would encourage me to go to college. Philosophy? Why would I want to go to school and philosophize about life? All I'd been doing for the past month was philosophizing. I had decided human nature was unpredictable: If someone had warned me that I'd be in this situation and asked me how I'd respond, my answer would have been wrong. I wouldn't have had a clue without living it.

Maybe psychology would be the major for me. I could study how the will to live is greater than the will to die— fascinating. No, no, college was not for me. I didn't know what I'd do. Anyway, now was not the time for making decisions about the future. Now was the time to persevere through each minute, and concentrate on surviving.

I never let myself drink a beer before sundown. Sometimes the sea melted into a sheet of glass at dusk. I'd crawl up on the boom, light a cigar, and pop open a Hinano. This was the loneliest time of day. How many sunsets had I enjoyed with Richard? We used to play a word game: describing the sunset in exact colors. Words like violet, cream, and chartreuse were easy—common. Richard might describe a sunset as "flax with a hint of mandarin, blended with carnelian and absinthe." I would giggle, watching him cop an attitude as he pronounced his witty description. My best had been, "The vermilionette sun dispersed its petal pink hues to primrose, parrot green, and plum over the wispy garnet clouds."

"Bravo." Richard had laughed and applauded me.

How could I not ache with loneliness when the sky was once again flax with hints of mandarin and my Richard wasn't there anymore?

Sometimes during those lonely sunsets I'd talk to Richard—dare him to come to me. Other times I'd sing stupid songs. Songs with silly lyrics that repeated themselves ninety-nine times. I tried to sing upbeat songs, not songs with lyrics of home and love.

Back at the wheel, I adjusted my pillows and steered with my foot. I searched the sky for my constellation friends. As I sailed north I distinguished new constellations. I was pretty sure the hero Perseus was taking his stand in the sky now amid the Milky Way. Perseus holds Medusa's head in his left hand and his shield in his right. Perseus's goal is to rescue Andromeda, using Cetus the sea beast's help. I couldn't help but wish that Richard were Perseus and his goal were to rescue me.

When I couldn't keep my eyes open any longer, I lashed the wheel and crawled into the sleeping bag, hugging Richard's flowered shirt. Often I'd hold it up to my nose and take in deep breaths, conjuring up his scent. I could picture his loving face in my mind, and I'd whisper sweet nothings to the soft cotton. He'd whisper back how much he loved and missed me. In the first light of dawn I would still be hugging the shirt. Oh, how I loved that shirt, its teals and turquoises reminding me of the teal seas of the atolls. I remembered what a difficult time Richard and I had had finding the entrance to Taenga as we sliced through the teal sea on a perfect beam reach. Wouldn't I now love to have the tradewinds filling the genoa and mainsail, heeling us over a comfortable twelve degrees as we approached Taenga.

Mayaluga heeled on a perfect beam reach from Raroia to the atoll. After four hours I peered through the binoculars, searching for the entrance to Taenga. All I could see were giant waves crashing along reefs that ran its length. We sailed parallel to it well offshore, and then came about and sailed back.

Finally I made out a concrete pad located in the channel, on the opposite side of the breakers. Straining my eyes, I saw a few single-story buildings and a couple of bright splashes of color that must be local fares—houses. Most atoll villages are established somewhere inside the lagoon, but this one, Taenga, was located along its entrance.

On our third pass, a local man zoomed out in an aluminum runabout. He circled, waving for us to follow him. We would have preferred to wait for the slack tide or even the ebb, but we didn't want to miss the chance of following this good Samaritan. As we motored toward the vaporizing white water, I felt very apprehensive. "Richard, I don't know about this."

"Tami, the bloke wouldn't be waving us in if we couldn't make it. Buck up, love. It won't be as bad as it looks." So I bucked up.

As we came around the line of swells, I could see the channel. It had been hidden between the breakers. Richard pushed the accelerator forward, forcing the engine to full throttle. It was the only way to make it through the boiling five-knot current coming straight at us, a current that had the power to turn us 180 degrees in a heartbeat and drag us back out.

I kept my eyes focused on our guide. Never had I experienced such a precarious entrance.

Once inside the channel, away from the gnarly breakers, we throttled back, made ready docking lines and fenders, and crept up to the concrete dock. A couple of locals eagerly helped us tie up.

One man boarded *Mayaluga*. He was the leader of the village. We asked him in French for permission to walk the village and to sail to the other *motus*. Motus are sandy islets chained together by underwater reefs that make up the circular or horseshoe-shaped atolls. He was pleased that we had asked permission and graciously gave it. Seeing we were eager to go ashore, he disembarked with us. He pointed to the path and waved us on to explore. We thanked him and eagerly went trekking through the small village. We didn't have to give our precious possessions on *Mayaluga* a second thought, as theft is unthinkable in the Tuamotus.

The village was immaculate. The walkways, meticulously lined with crushed coral and rocks, wound attractively around the village proper, veering off to the various homes. At the residences, the paths narrowed but continued in their tidy and defined way up to uneven wooden stairs and listing porches. It felt good to walk and sightsee.

Back on *Mayaluga* we pushed away from the dock, adjusted the sails for a head wind, and made our way to the windward side of the atoll.

About halfway across the lagoon we reached a huge coral head standing well above the surface of the water. We took all sail down and let the boat drift while we snorkeled in the aquamarine water around the magnificent complex ecosystem. Its porous surface snapped, crackled, and popped with life as reef and sergeant major fish darted about. We watched a two-foot rainbow parrotfish—one of the largest coral-eating herbivores—make the rounds. My favorite fish at the coral head forest was the pearly razor fish—I liked the contrast of its milky, light fuchsia color sparkling in the turquoise sea.

Refreshed from our swim, we hoisted the sails again and headed for a motu whose outline looked like a turtle's back. We named the small islet "Turtle Back Island" and stayed a few days. I spent hours and hours collecting shells along the lagoon side of the motu. Richard windsurfed, and we snorkeled a couple of times a day, always with the dinghy at our side. Most of the time we didn't even put on our bathing suits. It was as if we were the only people on earth.

Each day we walked across the motu to explore the fantastic barrier reefs on the ocean side. We carried our machetes along the cavernous sienna reef, keeping an eye out for eels as we strolled sometimes in ankle-deep water, along the prickly, curved slabs of petrified coral.

White water from breaking waves came rushing across the coral and crawled up our boots, then slurped away from us, back out to sea, only to return. As the tide receded we could hear air being sucked down holes in the hollow areas of the reef; within a few seconds the vapors would explode in the air with huge fountains of saltwater—such magnificent blowholes.

Coral heads loomed out of the reef like giant sculptures. Each evening the sunset backlit these heads, creating mysterious silhouettes against the fire-lit sky. Amber, carnelian colors blazed across the horizon. We sat as totems, wrapped up in the awe of the magnificent sky, worshiping the gift of another day well spent.

We left Turtle Back in time to catch the slack tide out the entrance of Taenga and five hours later we anchored in the lagoon of the atoll Makemo, near its village. It wasn't long before we heard children shouting and splashing their way out to *Mayaluga*. As they reached the boat we looked down on twenty smiling faces, ranging in age from five to twelve, treading water around us. We invited them all on board, and they didn't hesitate to climb swiftly up the swim ladder. There was not an ounce of shyness in the bunch. They ran around the deck chattering enthusiastically. I showed them the interior of *Mayaluga* in groups of three and four. Our *pahi*—boat—was our fare—our house—I told them. When we were ready to go ashore, the kids jumped off the boat and swam to land, racing us as Richard pretended to row harder and harder to beat them. They won.

With help from our little friends, we pulled the dinghy up on the beach and tied it to a *nui*—coconut tree.

One of the older kids volunteered to take us to the pearl farm. As we walked we admired the quaint multicolored fares along the way, with bright Tahitian flowered curtains hanging in the windows. The flora surrounding the homes was just as brilliant. Makemo appeared to be more lush with plants and blossoms than the other atolls we had visited.

The pearl farm was a one-story building with a concrete-slab dock on pilings. We walked in and noticed a small Asian man in a white lab coat peering through a magnifying glass into a giant *naka*—black-lip oyster. In each hand he had a long, thin utensil with a small scoop on the end. With one utensil he would scoop up what looked like sand, and with the other scoop up a gooey, clear activator. Placing the two in the naka apparently conceived the precious Polynesian black pearl. Another man came in, collected the primed mother-of-pearl shells, and took them to the shells' nesting ground somewhere in the lagoon.

We spent one clear and balmy night at Makemo. Sitting in the cockpit that evening, I felt peaceful and content. The sky glittered with stars surrounding the more-than-half-lit moon. Holding my right hand up to the moon, I aimed to caress the old man's illustrious right cheek. Ah yes, a waxing moon when the full side fits in my right palm.

"Do you think a month will be enough time for us in Tahiti?"

"I don't know; I've been thinking about that too," Richard admitted.

"Bastille Day is only twenty days away."

"I'd hate to miss Tahiti's celebration of the fall of the Bastille in Paris, but more so, I'd hate to miss those canoe races along the waterfront. Do you think the quay will get crowded?"

"Yes," I replied.

"You do?"

"Every sailor in the vicinity goes to the Bastille Day festival," I said.

Richard held his right hand up to the moon. "He'll be full within the week. Maybe we should leave for Papeete tomorrow."

"Are you ready for the big city?" I teased.

"I'm ready for a good steak and kidney pie."

"I don't know if you'll find the two together in Papeete."

"But surely I can find all the ingredients and make one myself."

"I'm sure you can. In fact, I think you're going to be able to find more things than you ever imagined in Papeete," I said, laughing.

"Good. Then shall we leave on the morrow?"

"The morrow it is."

FIFTEEN

In Broad Daylight

Day Thirty-Four after the capsize, with an estimated 240 miles to go, I was savoring my last can of sardines when—just like that—a ship came out of nowhere. Throwing down the can of sardines, I jumped up to get to the flares. I was so frantic, I tripped in the cockpit and fell, almost breaking my leg. I hobbled over to the watertight container in which the flare gun and flares were stored and tore off the lid. I took hold of the loaded gun, held it in the air and shot. *BAM!*

"I'm home! I'm almost home. Oh, God, what will I say? I wonder if they're American?" I babbled as I loaded another flare and shot it off.

Hold it, girly-girl. You're not home yet.

BAM! went another flare. "Oh yes I am. There! See? The ship sees me." It looked as if the ship were altering course and heading toward me. I ran back to the wheel, snatched up my pareu, and put it on. I grabbed the container of flares and picked up the oar with the red T-shirt tied onto it, and started madly waving the oar as I did a jig. "I'll be in Hawaii tonight. A haole's delight. All bathed and bright. No more fright."

"Wait a minute!" I shouted.

I dropped the oar and shot off another flare. Then I shot off a parachute flare and a second parachute flare.

"You can't leave. Why are you leaving?" I yelled at the distant silhouette of the ship. "What can I do? I've got to stop them."

I found the mirror stashed in the mizzenmast binnacle and with the help of the sun started flashing signals.

The ship had never altered course; it must have been an optical illusion or just my deep, deep desire to be found.

All I could do was stomp around the deck screaming obscenities: "God damn it! This is insane. Here I am in broad daylight and you can't even see me. You stupid ship! Couldn't you see the stupid flares?" With that, I grabbed a winch handle and started beating on the boom until I could pound no longer. I dropped the winch handle and picked up my half-eaten can of sardines and threw them overboard. I collapsed in the cockpit, sobbing.

"This is crazy. I'm crazy."

You're not crazy.

"I am too," I screamed to the sky.

You just counted your chickens before they hatched.

"I thought they saw me."

Yes, you're right, they should have. Hold on, love. You're almost there.

Even though I was thinking it, I could not say it out loud

or The Voice would annihilate me. But I wished with all my heart that we had never left Tahiti. I knew there was no point in thinking it, but I couldn't stop myself. My nostrils tingled with the humid smell of saltwater mist. How soon would I smell land again—deep, dark dirt, with its richly pungent aroma? I recalled when Richard and I first saw the volcanoes of the Society Islands and how when approaching Tahiti the wind carried the essence of land. . . .

"Richard, I smell the earth. Do you?"

Richard sniffed the air deeply and smiled. "Bloody right, love. I never thought the land of volcanoes could smell so sweet, so fertile."

"It's all the flowers. The frangipani and gardenia thrive in the humidity. They're the flowers of love, you know. I'll get you a lei, love."

"I'd love a lei, love."

The anticipation of the hustle-bustle of Tahiti, after spending so much time in remote villages, was thrilling. The idea of reaching land and the little pleasures to come, like going to the bureau de poste for our mail and eating hamburgers and fries, tantalized us. Calling home would be a treat. I looked forward to hearing the latest gossip of who's doing what with whom, and how much everybody missed us. But our first order of business would be to check into customs. It didn't matter that we had originally checked into Hiva Oa three months ago. Tahiti is not part of the

Marquesan Islands group or the Tuamotu Archipelago, but rather it is one of the Windward Islands of the Society Islands group. French Polynesia is comprised of these three island groups.

As we came into Papeete's harbor, our whole world changed in a matter of moments. Gas and diesel fumes tinged the air. Activity surrounded us. We motored around to get our bearings and put the dinghy in the water. Then, selecting a spot on the quay, we backed in, aligning *Mayaluga* parallel to the rest of the boats.

"Ahoy, *Mayaluga,*" came an enthusiastic shout from the quay. "How was your trip?"

"Fantastic," Richard yelled to Jean Pierre, the owner of *Rashaba,* a steel sloop that housed a family of four we had met in the Marquesas.

With the electronics shut down and our sailing gear stowed, we collected our passports and the boat's papers, pulled the stern line in, and jumped on shore.

The paved road, Boulevard Pomme, ran parallel to the quay. The noise of speeding cars, mopeds, bikes, and people intimidated us somewhat, yet excited us too.

"My God," Richard said, "this place is a zoo."

The customs office was close by. We walked right in and handed over our passports to the stern-faced official. All of our personal papers and *Mayaluga's* papers were in order, showing our bond had been posted in Hiva Oa. Checking in was once again a breeze. Now we were anxious to eat.

The boulevard was lined with *les roulettes,* small trucks,

like catering trucks, that specialize in certain foods. Crossing
the street we were torn by which roulette to eat at first. There
were crepes, stir-fry over noodles, chicken and rice, ice cream,
and hamburgers, as well as steaks and fries, shish kebab—you
name it.

"Man, it smells good," I said. "The first thing I'm going to
get is a brochette."

"What's a brochette?"

"A shish kebab."

"That sounds great. But I'm dying for a steak." Richard
smiled and licked his lips.

I ate one shish kebab, a crepe, and a double-decker chocolate chip mint ice-cream cone. Richard ate twice as much as I
did. We felt like slugs when we finished.

At the post office we mailed the letters we had written on
our way to Papeete from Makemo and collected eight letters
from our general delivery address. Thrilled to have received
so much mail, we decided not to call home until we had read
the letters. We'd read them on *Mayaluga,* where we could
relax, and then call home the next day.

At a supermarket we picked up some sesame crackers as
well as a choice brie from the rows and rows of fresh cheese,
and Richard spotted a merlot he swore I'd love. Walking back
toward the boat, we stopped in at the open-air market for
some tomatoes, a red onion, and apples.

Kicked back in the cockpit sipping the smooth, fruity
merlot, I opened the earlier of two letters from my mom. Aha,
she had met a man named Brian through some friends, and
they had a lot in common, she said, because he also worked

on boats. Only he did mechanical and electrical repair. She added that the brightwork business she had taken over from me was doing great.

My mom's second letter was posted two weeks after the first. She and Brian were planning a trip on his boat to Catalina. She wrote, "He could be the one." Good for Mom, I thought.

Richard opened a letter from his sister, Susie, and then one from his dad. His sister hoped we were well and not so distracted by our love that we'd make navigational mistakes! His father wrote that he was checking the atlas daily to visualize *Mayaluga*'s progress. He hoped we hit fair winds and didn't get stuck too long in the doldrums. He wanted Richard to be sure to call as soon as we arrived in Tahiti. Richard smiled as he folded up the letter and put it away.

The letter from my dad said my little brother was growing like a weed and Carolyn, my stepmother, was busy trying to keep up with the little rascal. He went on to say the waves had been great and he had been getting some surfing in on his days off from the fire department.

I could tell my grandparents' letter from my grandmother's perfect handwriting. A lot of company from the Midwest had been visiting, she wrote—everybody loved California because of its good weather. They hoped the cruise was easy and told me to be sure and call collect when I got to a phone. P.S., she added, Say hello to Richard.

Dan, the guy who had crewed with me delivering the racing yacht to San Francisco, had also written a letter with Sandra, his wife. Richard opened their letter next. They were envious, wishing they were in French Polynesia instead of San Diego. They had decided to move to the desert.

"The desert?" I questioned Richard as he read.

"That's what the old sod wrote. He says they are going to open a store and sell sunglasses."

We burst out laughing. Guess it makes sense to sell sunglasses in the desert.

The next day we called home. Everyone was as glad to hear our voices as we were to hear theirs. There's nothing like touching home base to warm the heart. My grandma said she was baking chocolate bread pudding for Grandpa, and I swear I could smell it over the phone.

We spent several days at the quay, beam to beam with the other yachts. Every day we went to the post office to check for and to send mail. We spent hours in the open-air market, buying fresh fruit and vegetables, wanting one of everything and knowing there would be no way to eat it all. We even bought flowers for *Mayaluga*'s table.

And what a thrill to get blocks of ice and have cold milk on corn flakes in the morning with lots of sugar. I loved the smell of ice in the icebox as I lifted the lid, the chill of the air stinging my nostrils. Ice was a luxury and, as every sailor without refrigeration knows, was nothing to be taken for granted!

A couple of boats Richard and I had met in the Marquesas were lined up along the quay: *Fleur d'ecosse,* owned by Anne and Ronald Falconer; and *Skylark,* owned by Phil and Betty Perish. Whenever a captain and mate felt in the mood, they would invite the other sailors over for potluck. A mélange of our private time together: Too often it seemed someone was yelling down from the quay, "Ahoy, *Mayaluga*," or rowing up and knocking on the hull, asking for "permission to come aboard."

We decided to go around to the quiet anchorage at Maeva Beach. Even though a huge hotel was located there, we knew it would still be more private than the quay.

Ten boats were moored at Maeva Beach when we pulled in. We dropped anchor, and both of us sighed deeply as the tranquility embraced us.

Not long after we arrived at Maeva Beach, Richard was asked to help repair a boat built with a ferro-cement hull like *Mayaluga*'s. Because he liked to keep busy and add to the cruising fund when opportunity knocked, he readily agreed. While Richard was at work, I painted *Mayaluga*'s interior and varnished her brightwork.

One day when Richard was rowing to work, he noticed a new boat in the bay. It was flying a British flag and her name was *Hazana*. Richard rowed closer and yelled a "tally-ho" to her owners. He told them he was the owner of *Mayaluga*, the other Brit boat in the bay. *Hazana*'s owners, Peter and Christine Crompton, were from Southampton, England, it turned out, which basically made them neighbors to Richard's family in Cornwall.

The Cromptons invited us for a drink late one afternoon. As we rowed up to *Hazana,* I was awed by her lines and size. She was a beautiful forty-four-foot Trintella, a ketch of van de Stadt's design, built by Anne Wever in Holland. Richard

unusual *bonnes bouches* (treats) appeared; sailing stories grew like fish stories.

Every evening the big canoes were launched at the waterfront to practice for the big race on Bastille Day. There were men's and women's teams, plus a relay team. The canoes sat twelve paddlers each. Richard and I would sit in the cockpit watching them practice around the harbor, and one evening Richard asked if he could go on a short jaunt if they had room for an extra man. They did, and when they dropped him off he was exhausted. "They're animals, love. Endurance like I've never seen."

A few days before Bastille Day the energy in the town crackled like lightning. Competitors from all over French Polynesia arrived, as did vendors who set up booths for selling their local cuisine.

Music accompanied the sunrise on Bastille Day. All the artists and merchants were set up in the square raring to sell their handmade quilts, paintings, carvings, tapas, baskets, jewelry, and food.

At the track, gunnysack races and horse races were taking place. Traditional Polynesian dance competitions went on throughout the day. Richard and I bought tickets to sit in the stands and watch the competition among the dancers, who performed all over the world. All their costumes were different, from palm-frond skirts, pom-poms and pom-pom headgear to bikini tops and waistbands intricately adorned with shells and beads. Other dancers wore shell crowns and pareus with leis over their bikini tops and flowers in their hair. All the dancers were sexy yet elegant, their hands signing a message that tantalized the mind. The Tamarii, a Tahitian dance, was especially sensual, with the men wildly flapping their knees and the women shaking their hips to and fro as they danced closer and closer.

Eventually Richard and I went down to the waterfront to watch the canoe races. Thousands of people had lined up to scream for their favorite teams, and we joined them, cheering for the team Richard had accompanied on his rowing jaunt.

Throughout the day on the waterfront we met up with our yachting buddies. We sat drinking beer and watching the vast variety of people walk by. We partied till the wee hours of the morning. And even when Bastille Day was over it took another couple of days for the partying to subside. Ah, the Tahitians really know how to celebrate.

—

As I came out of my Tahitian daydream, I breathed deeply, smelling the air, and glanced at the long lost wake of the ship that had dropped over the horizon, not seeing me. I decided I didn't care that The Voice thought I had counted my chickens before they hatched. I stood up and shouted like a loony-tune: "WE SHOULD HAVE NEVER LEFT TAHITI. DO YOU HEAR ME, RICHARD? WE—SHOULD—HAVE—NEVER—LEFT—THE—DIRT!"

I—HOPE—YOU—FEEL—BETTER—NOW, came the know-it-all Voice.

SIXTEEN

Hazana *and* Maeva Bea[c]

I was restless. Thinking back to the excitement of Bas[tille] Day in Tahiti and what fun we had left me feeling like a ca[ged] animal trapped here on *Hazana*. I had nowhere to go [but] around and around the deck. I tried to take deep breath[s to] calm down and relax. But all I smelled was the turbid s[cent] of saltwater mist, a scent that made me sick now. My m[ood] definitely did not fit the slow pace of traveling a mere [?] across this vast sea.

Tami, if you'll be honest with yourself, you'll remember [you] *and Richard were ready for the festival to be over.*

"You know, Voice, I didn't want it to end, I just wa[nted] some peace and quiet, but this is ridiculous."

After all the festivities of Bastille Day, Richard and I fi[rst] found the never-ending noise and traffic at the quay to b[e] overwhelming. We were partied out and decided we m[ust]

introduced me to Peter and Christine, and they gave us a tour of *Hazana*'s interior, which was adorned like a five-star hotel compared to our *Mayaluga*. The Cromptons were an attractive couple, mid-fifties, and very friendly, not pretentious at all. Peter made us a round of drinks, and we sat in the spacious cockpit enjoying the hors d'oeuvres Christine had made. Richard and the Cromptons learned they had a couple of acquaintances in common. We thoroughly enjoyed the visit.

A few days later the Cromptons asked us over for dinner. Much to Richard's delight, Christine added an English flare to the Polynesian meal with a homemade mango chutney. After dinner Christine mentioned her father was ill and that they were thinking of returning to England. Peter wondered what the possibilities might be of finding a delivery crew to sail *Hazana* to California, as it would be more convenient for them to come and go from the United States when they wanted to visit Christine's father. We could tell they were quizzing us about the delivery job. They asked what sailing experience we had, and we told them what we had done separately and together. They were amazed to learn that between us, Richard and I had sailed over fifty thousand miles.

Back on *Mayaluga* Richard asked me how I'd feel about delivering *Hazana*. At first I wasn't interested—we'd only been gone a few months and I wasn't ready to go back to the States. I wanted to keep traveling and make it to New Zealand before going home for a visit.

But Richard went ahead and told Peter we might be interested in delivering *Hazana* to San Diego—depending on the fee.

Richard and Peter met again and discussed the terms of *Hazana*'s delivery to San Diego, California. When Richard came home and told me we'd be paid ten thousand dollars and airline tickets—from San Diego to Europe, back to San Diego, and then back here to Tahiti—I perked up and instantly got interested in the job. It really did seem too good to pass up. We could cruise a long time on ten thousand dollars. Since I had never been to Europe the idea of spending Christmas in England sounded exciting. The Cromptons liked the idea of being back on *Hazana* for Christmas, which meant *Hazana* would not be left unattended once she reached the States. After England, Richard and I could fly to San Diego and then back to *Mayaluga* in Tahiti and continue on to New Zealand. What would four months be out of our lives? We agreed to deliver *Hazana*.

Peter and Christine made reservations to fly home. A couple of days before they left, we went through *Hazana* with them. Christine took me through the galley operations, showing me where cooking utensils were kept and food goods stored. Peter took Richard through the engine room, explaining *Hazana*'s little quirks and his personal preferences for treatment of the engine and electronic gear.

The next day we went back to *Hazana* and went through the topside gear, the sails and rigging. *Hazana* was a sophisticated boat with roller-furling headsails, self-tailing winches,

electric winches in the cockpit for the sheets—the lines—
and a hydraulic boom vang. I actually started getting excited
about our journey north aboard her. She was a Class-A boat.

Peter shook Richard's hand heartily when he handed over
Hazana's keys and said: "Have a good crossing and be safe."

"Not to worry, we'll treat her like our own," Richard
assured him, smiling.

The Cromptons were all packed, their bags lined up on
a seat locker. Richard helped Peter load the bags in their
dinghy, which they motored to shore, and we rowed behind
them in our dinghy. Once on shore there were hugs good-bye
and a promise: "We'll see you in San Diego." The Cromptons
left for the airport.

Richard and I ran back down the beach where the din-
ghies were tied. I grabbed the line to the Cromptons' dinghy
before Richard. Noticing the disappointment on his face I
said, "just kidding," as I traded painters—lines—with him.
I knew he was eager to try out the inflatable with its fifteen
horsepower outboard.

Our friends Antoinette and Haipade agreed to watch *Mayaluga* for us while we were delivering *Hazana* to San Diego.
They were the couple I had met my first time through the
South Pacific. Haipade suggested we leave *Mayaluga* moored
in the small bay in front of their house in Mataiea. The bay
could only hold a couple of boats and would be a safe anchorage for *Mayaluga* while we were gone.

Richard plotted the course from Maeva Beach to the
private bay, timing our entry for a high slack tide. As we

rounded the point, we zigzagged our way into the narrow sliver of a channel.

Richard took special care to set the anchor. We stripped off all the sails and stowed them below. He drained the freshwater pump and the head and shut off all the thru-hull valves.

From the dinghy I watched Richard slide *Mayaluga*'s hatch shut. He patted the top of the hatch a couple of times and said, "We'll be back soon, love." Then he climbed down into the dinghy, untied the painter, and rowed us to shore.

Moving aboard *Hazana* was like moving into the honeymoon suite at a Hilton hotel. She had pressurized hot running water for showers and two heads on board. The galley was a gourmet cook's delight, with plenty of room below to move around in. She also had miles of foredeck space and a giant cockpit, not to speak of the latest in electronics.

We provisioned in Tahiti, planning for a thirty-day crossing to San Diego. There were leftovers from the Cromptons' provisioning, as well as the goods we had brought from *Mayaluga*. But now that we had refrigeration, we bought extra treats.

Richard returned to *Hazana* that afternoon carrying a large rectangular box, ornately wrapped. "What's that?" I asked curiously.

Handing the box to me and smiling broadly, he said, "Open it and see."

"Do you think it's my birthday?" I questioned.

"No."

"An anniversary?" I cringed, scanning my mind's personal calendar.

"No."

I pulled on the scarlet ribbon, and the box yawned partially open. Lifting the lid, a mossy green hue glowed under thin ivory paper. Unfolding the tissue, I lifted out a slinky spaghetti-strapped dress. "For me?"

"Do you like it?"

"It's gorgeous," I purred as I stood and held the dress against me. It was a seafoam green silk that was tapered at the waist and hit just above my knees. "But why?"

"For being you," he simply stated.

When I looked puzzled, he continued. "I saw it on a mannequin in a shop window. She looked just like you, waist-length blond hair, green eyes the color of glass, and a perfect body. I knew it was meant for you."

Blushing, I said, "You're something else," and threw my arms around him, smothering him with kisses.

"Come on, let's get cleaned up. I've made dinner reservations at Le Belvedere. Should we walk or take a cab?" he asked.

"Le Belvedere—wow. Let's walk. I want to show off my new dress."

The late afternoon heat spiraled up from the roadway. We walked as much in the shade as we could, enjoying the breeze that gently blew against our skin. I felt like a million bucks in my new dress. We trekked into a valley and along a lush canyon that must have contained every shade of green ever created.

The restaurant's covered patio overlooked a spectacular

canyon populated with exotic trees, shrubs, and flowers. In the distance spread the frothy rolling sea.

Dinner was scrumptious. Very rich with coconut cream and butter. When the table was cleared Richard reached across and took my hand. I watched him fondle my fingers and then I looked into his eyes, seeing that candid blue gaze.

"I love you with all my heart, Tami. And I want to be with you forever."

"I hope so," I answered, smiling, feeling a bit self-conscious as I wondered about the purpose of his confession.

"Will you marry me?" he suddenly blurted out, slipping an intricately knotted white twine ring on my finger.

"It's lovely. Did you make it?"

"Yes. When we arrive back in the States I'll get you the real thing. Whatever you'd like."

I shook my head no. "Nothing can ever be as precious as this." My eyes brimmed.

"What's wrong? Don't you want to marry me?"

"Yes—yes, I want to marry you. I'd marry you this second."

"Jeez, Tami, for a minute I thought you were going to say no."

"No? Are you crazy? I'd be crazy to say no."

We strolled back to *Hazana*, stopping to enjoy long slow kisses. I wondered out loud how my new name, Mrs. Richard Sharp, would sound. Or Tami Sharp. Or Richard and Tami Sharp. Richard said, "It sounds just right."

Back on *Hazana* we turned on slow music and danced for a spell in each other's arms. I suddenly felt like a woman, not a girl. A woman soon to be a wife. Romance rocked *Hazana* that night.

With *Hazana* ready to go, we were too. There was nothing left to do, we contemplated leaving Tahiti early for the crossing to California. We had studied the weather reports carefully: No storms were forecast, so we felt pretty confident we would be safe as far as the weather was concerned. We estimated we could make good time sailing from the southern hemisphere into the northern hemisphere, and as it was past the middle of hurricane season and the occurrence of storms at this time of the year was statistically low, we decided to go for it. We felt indestructible—we knew our love could conquer all.

We left Moorea and went back to Papeete to top off the fuel, water, and propane tanks. We checked out of Papeete at 1330 hours, September 22. As *Mayaluga* was remaining in Tahiti, and we were returning within four months, our bonds remained posted. We took off for America.

SEVENTEEN

Glow Sticks and Milkshakes

It was Day Thirty-Five. I estimated I was still 145 miles from Hawaii. I was starting to see floating objects—signs of humanity like plastic soda-pop bottles, a tattered tarp, flip-flops, and a Styrofoam float.

I used battery power only at night, to light up the two cockpit compasses—one in the binnacle at the wheel, the other on the cockpit bulkhead. One of *Hazana*'s two batteries had been thrown out of its Plexiglas casing during the capsize, but by a miracle it had landed right side up, undamaged. If it had landed any other way, I probably would have been painfully, perhaps fatally, burned by acid-contaminated water before I came to. The other battery, still in its casing, was also undamaged.

When the first battery finally ran out of juice, I switched to the second one, realizing it might also give out before I reached safety. To conserve battery power I started using glow sticks, which I had found while cleaning below.

That night I cracked my first one. The lime green light crackled like magic in my hand. It reminded me of when I was a kid and we'd go to the beach at night to see the slender, silvery grunion run. Waves would cast the grunion on shore and we'd run up and down the soft wet sand waving our glow sticks like pirates wave their swords.

Sometimes I would sneak away from the other kids and hide near the pier at the water's edge. I'd let my feet sink in the sand, imagining it to be quicksand until I felt that first crusty edge of a sand crab's claw. Then I'd leap back and run for my life, screaming at the top of my lungs, "The crabs are coming. The crabs are coming." I'd run as fast as I could past the other children, and sure enough, they'd start screaming and running too.

Holding the glow stick up to the starless night, I started writing in the sky. I wrote Richard's name, over and over and over. I scribbled a rolling *R*, with a flourish at the end of the *D*.

Facing the bow and pointing the wand straight ahead, I commanded: "Love—come to me." And slowly brought the wand to my heart. Turning starboard I grasped the wand to my heart and repeated my order, "Come to me." Feeling the wind freshen on my left cheek, I checked the compass and altered course a degree. I did an about-face to the stern and the path I had just traveled, and said in a deep voice, "Richard, let your spirit come to me." Gracefully turning portside, I stretched my right arm out as far as I could, and then gradually brought the wand to my breast, repeating the mantra: "Come to me."

I set the glow stick on top of the binnacle. I glanced

at my heading and shifted the wheel a couple of degrees. Feeling omnipotent, I expanded my commands: "Bring me a milkshake. It has to be from Baskin-Robbins, you know, thirty-one flavors, and it must be chocolate chip mint." The craving became too much, and the spell broke. "Oh man, what I wouldn't do for a milkshake right now."

Stop it. Don't be ridiculous. You know you can't have a milkshake.

"Haven't you ever wanted a milkshake?"

Of course I have. But this fantasy is pointless.

"Maybe you have no imagination."

Maybe I don't like to put myself through unnecessary longings.

The Voice had no sense of humor, I discovered. I pretended to drink my chocolate chip mint milkshake. "Ummm. Oh man, this is good. Ummm. I can hardly stand how refreshing the mint makes my mouth feel."

Cool?

"Very cool."

The Voice hesitated. *May I have some?*

"Sorry, it's all gone," I said, tossing the invisible cup overboard.

Oh, man . . .

"Next time you should grasp the joy of fantasy."

———

For the next few days the wind was fluky. I cursed the devil for this.

Don't allow the devil into your thoughts, Tami, said The Voice.

"Why, are you afraid of the devil?"

Only a fool isn't afraid of the devil.

A chill went through me. "What should I think about?"

Think about your destination.

Then on Day Thirty-Eight, with the sun blazing in the sky, I couldn't stay under the blanket any longer—I was boiling. I had been awake most of the night, steering and thinking about my destination. If only I could sleep in, have breakfast in bed.

I sat up and stretched. As I headed for the bow to check the rig, I looked around and stopped short. "It can't be—can it?" I squinted, trying to focus. "It's got to be."

On the horizon I saw an isolated cloudlike shape. At first light I thought it was low cumulus clouds. But by noon the mass became a granite-colored smudge in front of me. Could it be Hawaii? I went back to the wheel, and for an hour I steered toward the increasingly defined land mass afraid to believe it was land and afraid to believe it wasn't. My heart pounded with a steady surge of fueled anticipation. Finally I believed it was terra firma—I was seeing land—I couldn't deny it, it had to be the island. Hawaii was right where I thought it should be. A great relief flooded over me. My spine seemed to melt as I held my head in my hands and cried.

After a short while I calmed down and was overcome by a feeling of awe. But what exactly am I in awe of, I wondered. Land? People? Home? Could it just be the reality that lay in front of me? Yes, everything I had been wanting was here. Well, almost everything . . . Suddenly excitement rushed through me, and I stood up and shouted: "LAND—

LAND HO!" Then I danced about like a warrior, quickly wearing myself out. "This calls for a celebration. Beer! My last beer, the one I've been saving for this moment. And a cigar. YAHOO!"

Scrambling below I sought out the beer and a cigar. Topside, I climbed on the boom, lit the cigar, and popped open the bottle. "Oh God, I'm so excited. And grateful. I'm so very, very grateful. Thank you. Mauruuru. Thank you. Amen." I hadn't felt grateful for anything in over a month, well, except for the fresh water, cigars, beer, and moisturizer. It felt good to suddenly feel so excited, so eager.

"I know my mom will come and get me. My parents will help with all this." But what can they really do? I thought. Hold my hand? It will be up to me to get organized, to notify everyone, to try to explain how it happened—why it happened. My positive feeling waned.

"What will I tell Richard's family?" Fear gripped me. "How will I tell them?" I involuntarily shook my head. "How will I be able to tell anyone about Richard?" Emotion choked me.

"And the Cromptons, this beautiful boat of theirs." *Hazana*, poor *Hazana*. *Hazana*, who saved my life. The Cromptons will be devastated too. "I'm sorry," I rehearsed, growing sadder. "We did our best. We did." They'll just have to believe me. Tears streamed down my face. "I've done my best too, really I have." The last drop of the hot beer muffled another sob.

"Oh God, what are people going to think of me? Look at me—I'm a wreck. I've lost so much weight, and my hair—my hair used to be so pretty. If one person looks at me funny, I'm gonna crack. I'm on a thin keel as it is. Oh God, I'm so scared."

My stomach suddenly felt nauseous. I was afraid to see people again, to get back into society. What was going on? Was I getting used to this solitary confinement? Did I want to stay out here forever, drifting into oblivion? Maybe it would be easier than explaining how it was that I lived and Richard got sucked into the bowels of the sea. His parents will wish I had been the one at the wheel. My parents, though sad, will be glad I wasn't. Will anyone realize it would have been better if both of us had died?

You're regressing. You were NOT meant to die. How many times do I have to tell you, Richard's time was up and yours is not. Just know everyone will be glad you are home and safe.

The Voice was like a warm blanket thrown over my shoulders. I wanted to believe The Voice; I needed to believe The Voice. "I'm so scared."

I know you are. And you have every right to be.

"You wouldn't be scared."

I might be. But one thing I know for sure is that I'd be happy I was not going to be alone anymore.

"I'm happy for that. Really, I am."

You're not acting happy. Dry those eyes. That's a girl.

"I suppose you'll leave me now too."

No, I will never leave you. I'm always here when you need me.

"Where do you live?"

I live in your soul.

"Like a soul mate? Or guardian angel?"

Yes, something like that.

The Voice and I sat quietly for a while. I felt totally at peace. Finally I sighed and announced: "Well, there's not a breath of wind up here to steer by; guess I better get her shipshape." And with that I crawled down off my perch and went below.

EIGHTEEN

De Plane — Me Insane?

Down below, *Hazana* didn't look shipshape by any means, but it was the best I could do. I was sitting at the chart table and had just finished writing in the logbook that I wished Richard could have been here with me to experience the relief of seeing the island, when I heard an engine. "What the . . ." I clambered topside.

Shading my eyes I looked around. The sound was coming from the sky; a plane. A military plane. A low-flying military plane! As quickly as I could, I shot off four flares. I grabbed the oar with the red T-shirt on it and waved and waved. The plane never even dipped its wing. I felt stunned. How in the hell could it not see me? Where's the island? All of a sudden the island was gone. "Where's the damn island?"

I looked at the palms of my hands and turned them over.

They looked like hands. I put my palms up to my cheeks and felt my face. It felt like a face. I licked the fingers of my right hand and rubbed my thumb over them. It was wet—sort of sticky. All of a sudden I slapped myself in the face. First with my right hand and then with my left. I kept slapping myself, until finally I screamed at the top of my lungs, "AHHHHHH-HHHHHHH! I'M DEAD, I'M DEAD. IT'S ALL A TRICK! I'VE BEEN DEAD ALL ALONG."

My knees gave way, and I collapsed onto the seat locker. "This is hell. I'm in hell. Hell, is this limbo? Is this the devil's trick? Not knowing what's real? I'm not real. No one sees me. No one saves me. It's going to be like this forever. What did I do that was so bad? All I did was go below like Richard told me. It's not my fault."

Standing up, I waved my fist at the heavens. "DO YOU HEAR ME, GOD? IT'S NOT MY FAULT. I'M SICK OF ALL THE GUILT. YOU MADE THE HURRICANE. YOU KILLED RICHARD. AND YOU MADE ME SURVIVE. HOW COULD YOU? WHAT IS SO MERCIFUL ABOUT YOU, GOD, THAT YOU KILLED RICH-ARD AND PUT ME IN THIS HELLHOLE? WELL, I'LL TELL YOU SOMETHING, I'M NOT STAYING HERE. I'M GOING TO SHOOT MY BRAINS OUT. THEN I WON'T BE ABLE TO WORRY ABOUT A GODDAMNED THING. TO HELL WITH THIS NIGHTMARE AND TO HELL WITH YOU!"

Hysterically, I dashed below and rummaged through the locker, grabbing the rifle. I gripped the towel and rolled the gun out onto a cushion. A box of shells fell out too. I loaded the rifle and, leaning against the nav station, tried to cram the barrel into my mouth. The cold metal cracked against my teeth. "Ouch. Come on, damn it."

I moved toward the settee, thinking that maybe if I sat down I wouldn't shake so much and the metal wouldn't rattle so violently against my teeth.

Tami, you know you can't take your own life now.

"WHAT ARE YOU TALKING ABOUT?" I slammed the butt of the rifle down on the floor frame. "I'M DEAD. I'M ALREADY DEAD! IT'S JUST MY BRAIN THAT ISN'T DEAD. MY IMAGINATION IS GOING ON AND ON AND ON. THERE IS NO RELIEF! I CAN'T STAND IT ANYMORE."

Tami, you're close. You're so close. Believe in yourself. Remember the prayer you love about God's big sea and your small boat. Tami, your boat is small, it IS hard to see. You know that. Put the rifle down. Believe in yourself. Don't give up the ship, girl. Go look. I dare you. Come on, I double dare you. The island IS real, it's not an illusion. It IS Hawaii. You're almost there. I promise—I promise. Go look—please, go look.

Chagrined, I let the rifle drop and leaped topside. The island was there, bright and clear.

"Oh my God, what did I almost do?" I clung to the boom to stop myself from shaking.

I almost gave up. I almost killed myself. I'm just so tired and lonely, I'm going crazy.

Letting go of the boom, I climbed down into the cockpit. I plunged my hands into the five-gallon bucket of saltwater and splashed big scoops of the cool water over my face.

"Oooh." It felt good. Not cold, but wet and real. I did it

again. Then I stretched my arms high, and as I lowered them I roared like a lioness: "AAAAAAAAAAAAAAAHHHHH!"

Staring at the island, my mind worked overtime: Believe in yourself, Tami. You heard The Voice. You made it this far. You don't need anyone or anything to save you. You must keep the faith, trust The Voice, and know there's a reason you lived.

I sat there for a moment, feeling my nerves unfray before I had to finally agree: "I was meant to save myself."

NINETEEN

Hold On, Hold On

That night I woke up to a heavy rain and building wind. The compass needle was all over the place. All I could do was keep the wheel lashed and pull a waterproof cover over me and my cockpit bed, and go back to sleep. I was exhausted.

When I was able to take my first sight the next day, my plotting showed I had been set north, pushed off my course by twenty-five miles. Traveling at two knots an hour, twenty-five miles was twelve hours. I had lost twelve hours!

I could no longer see the island. I made a conscious decision to stay awake and tend the wheel constantly. That night I went into the galley in search of a stimulant. The best I could come up with was a cold cocoa-coffee drink. I filled a thermos with the mixture and took it to the cockpit.

And so, on my forty-first day alone at sea I sailed to within a few miles of the entrance to Hilo Harbor. At 0230 in the morning the lights in the bay beckoned me, but I dared not go closer because of the huge reef that stretched far off shore. With a glow stick I studied the illustrated chart of Hilo Harbor I had found in an old cruising guide. The words "Not for navigational purposes" stood out. Oh, how I wanted to ignore them and get to those lights, some real food, real people, a shower, and some decent sleep. But only a fool or a sailor with local knowledge would attempt the hazardous entrance at night. I had to keep reminding myself that I hadn't gone through all this to end up on a reef now.

So, in the early morning I tacked back and forth just off the reef-strewn entrance. I was so near and yet still so agonizingly far away. Couldn't I just be there? No, I couldn't. I felt so confused. I knew I was a changed woman, never to be that innocent, carefree girl again. I was afraid of the humanity only a few miles away, yet excited too. Tears poured down my face.

"These tears—where are they coming from?" I asked The Voice.

These are different tears, Tami. These are tears of joy.

"But it's wrong to feel joy. I should be sad. I am still sad. I miss Richard so much."

You will always miss Richard, and you will always love Richard. But life goes on, Tami. You have to believe in yourself. Richard's time was up, and yours wasn't. You survived because you are you. Not everyone would have made it. Feel joy, you deserve it.

Soon you'll be with people who love you and you'll be smothered by all the love you've been missing.

"But it won't be the same."

It will be what you make of it. Another man will come when you are ready, and he will love you as deeply as Richard did.

"But will I be able to love him as much as I loved Richard?"

Yes. In time your heart will open and be eager to love again. Believe in yourself, in what your heart tells you.

"I'm going to miss you."

I'm always here, I'm a part of you.

"Are you God?"

The Voice never answered. Maybe there is no answer.

Early morning crept along slowly. I knew it would be my last few hours at sea, my last hours to be alone. I wondered who my first contact would be. A fishing boat? A private yacht?

Glancing to port, the pastel lights along the mountainside of Hilo, Hawaii, were beginning to go out one by one. Hold on Tami, hold on.

I couldn't help but ask myself again, as I had a million times already: Why? Why hadn't I realized we were vulnerable; that one or both of us could die out here in the middle of the ocean?

But the core of my being shouted back in defense: Because I was fearless—Richard was fearless. It was true I had fantasized about tropical isles and white, sandy beaches, warm water, perfect waves, exotic ports, and love.

I finally had to admit that nothing could have kept me from the sea.

I looked at my star friends in the sky and said a farewell to each constellation that had so delightfully entertained me and guided me on this long, slow voyage. The *W* in the sky was for water, but it still stood for *Wondrous* to me. Wondrous and wonderful Richard. Wondrous and wonderful that I had made it. I knew the stars would never be as outstanding on land as they are out here at sea.

I grabbed Richard's flowered shirt to my heart and desperately confessed: "I love you. You know I love you. I love you with all my heart." It was all I could say. I could not look at the lapis lazuli sea without seeing his eyes. I could not say that final good-bye. I stuffed his shirt inside mine, next to my heart, and reached for the twine ring on my finger that Richard had given me and twirled it and twirled it and twirled it.

≡

As dawn strolled aimlessly across the sky, I took a deep breath and readied *Hazana* for the harbor entry.

At the bow I heaved the anchor out of its locker and then pulled all the chain onto the deck. I wanted the anchor and chain ready to drop overboard to anchor *Hazana* in case she drifted too close to the reef or shore.

I hoisted the American red, white, and blue on the left side of the jury rig's shroud as a courtesy, and then automatically hoisted the yellow quarantine flag below it as all sailors learn to do when crossing international waters and entering a new port. I dug out, from down below, *Hazana*'s home-port flag: England. As I unfurled it, I tried to brush out the mildew and wrinkles. I thought how stately this flag of red, white, and blue is too. I liked how the plus mark and the cross dissected the blue into eight sections. I stuck the flag in its holder on the stern rail, remembering how proud Richard was of his citizenship.

I went back to the wheel and altered course for the harbor entrance. No sooner had I done this than I noticed a large ship heading out of the harbor entrance. I grabbed the flare gun and started shooting.

The ship seemed to pause.

I shot off a couple more flares and then grabbed the oar with the faded red T-shirt. At the bow, I waved it evenly back and forth, not frantically as I had all the unsuccessful times before.

Suddenly the vessel flashed its running lights and altered course.

My God, they see me. They actually see me. I didn't know what to do. I felt as if I should do something, but what? They were approaching fast. What will I say? "Hello, my name is Tami Oldham, and this is the sailing yacht *Hazana*. I've been like this for a long time. . . ."

Hazana started to rock as the looming ship reversed its engines and slowed down, sending forward its bow wake. I was afraid it would ram me. It was huge, two hundred feet or so. It cast a dark shadow over *Hazana*. Faces of Asian, Poly-nesian, and American men and women were peering over the rail intently staring down at me. I felt exposed and vulnerable. Suddenly, one of the crewmen on board shouted at me through the loudspeaker. I could barely hear him through the rumble of the engines now grumbling in neutral gear. "ARE YOU ALL RIGHT?" he yelled.

I nodded yes and then burst out crying. Through my sobs I saw the pity in the eyes watching me. I heard some shouts and, looking up, saw nodding heads and smiles of encouragement. "IT'S OKAY. WE'LL HELP YOU. YOU'LL BE FINE," shouted the spokesperson.

As I regained control of myself, I heard him ask: "HAS SOMEONE DIED?"

Again, I nodded yes.

"IS THAT THE BODY?" questioned the officer, pointing to the orange inflatable dinghy rolled up and lashed down on the port aft-quarter.

Baffled, I shook my head no.

"WE'VE NOTIFIED THE COAST GUARD. DO YOU NEED ANYTHING?"

I needed everything—Richard most of all. But I shook my head no and grasped the bow pulpit harder to keep from falling overboard from *Hazana*'s rough rolling in the ship's wake.

Soon someone swung a glass container, tied on a line, down to me from the deck of the vessel. I nodded my thank-you. Untying it proved very difficult with my weak and nervous hands. I could smell the hot coffee before I tasted it. I set it down to catch the apple someone else wanted to throw me. It seemed like forever since I had tasted an apple. As I bit into it, the sweet juice rolled down my chin. It made me cry all over again, for it tasted sweeter than I remembered a fresh apple could.

It was a great effort for the large vessel to go in and out of gear; to stay close yet far enough away from *Hazana*. It had been standing by for what seemed like forever, waiting for the Coast Guard.

"WE'RE GOING TO PASS YOU A TOWLINE," came an announcement suddenly.

There was a shout from up above, and then a "monkey's fist" was thrown down to me. I held out my arm to snare the casted line, then pulled in all the excess, finally reaching the hawser attached to it. The hawser was huge—two inches in diameter. I could barely get it on board; it weighed a ton. It was the type of rope you'd use to tow another huge ship, not a svelte sailboat. I couldn't decide where to tie the monstrosity. Finally I wrapped it around the anchor windlass. Once it was secured, I yelled "Go SLOW—SLOW!" and waved my hands, palms down, in front of me.

As the ship's engines roared, I held on tight. *Hazana* jerked forward. The fiberglass cover on the anchor windlass crunched into pieces, but the windlass itself held by two of its four bolts. Soon we seemed to be galloping across the swells. The slowest the ship could go was probably the fastest *Hazana* had ever gone. We were moving at least ten knots in nothing flat. It took all my concentration to steer *Hazana* behind the ship. I could sense all the faces watching me. All I could think was, Stay on track—stay on track, don't panic now.

Retrieving the towline

The ship towed me inside the reef and stopped. The ebbing current kept *Hazana* from running into it. Soon the Coast Guard Auxiliary arrived in their twenty-six-foot boat. I cast off the ship's hawser and then secured the lines the Coast Guard Auxiliary crew had thrown to me. *Hazana* was now side-tied to the rail of the Coast Guard Auxiliary runabout.

Inside Radio Bay was a concrete quay. The Coast Guard Auxiliary towed me to it, and I tied up to another Coast Guard boat moored there. Then two Coast Guard officials came on board. One was Petty Officer Rodenhurst. I kept crying and couldn't talk in complete sentences. He was exceptionally kind to me. I'm sure I was in shock.

Also moored at the quay was the blue-hulled sloop *Tamarii*, which Richard and I had seen in the Marquesas. As I

Hazana tied to the quay at Radio Bay, Hilo, Hawaii

glanced its way, I could see its owners watching the Coast Guard tow me in. The woman, Helga, yelled to me, "WHEN YOU'RE DONE, COME OVER TO OUR BOAT."

Petty Officer Rodenhurst gently suggested to me a number of times that they had a shower I could use. I needed a shower, but I wasn't ready for the isolation. I needed human contact.

I was very anxious to go to *Tamarii* and talk to fellow cruisers, or at least to people I felt I could relate to and who could relate to me and Richard. I gave the Coast Guard men a condensed version of what had happened, enough for them to get the picture and that there was no way I needed an ambulance or hospital. They told me they would need to take a written statement in a while, but to go ahead and visit my friends.

When I got to *Tamarii*, a feast awaited me. Eggs, ham,

roast beef, cheese, potato salad, sweetbreads, milk, juice, and coffee. I sat down and poured my heart out. I ate and cried, and cried and ate, and eventually laughed a time or two. The German couple were fascinated with my story. They asked me questions and I answered as we talked and talked. They offered me a cigarette, which I took, and gave me a snifter of brandy. All their nurturing helped to calm me, to feel at one with humanity again.

A couple hours had passed when Petty Officer Rodenhurst came knocking on the hull. "Tami, we need to take that statement now. Okay?"

I left *Tamarii* with more tears but with a newfound strength. "Would you like to get a change of clothes so you can shower?" Rodenhurst asked.

"Yes, yes . . ."

It wasn't until the hot water was streaming down my back that I realized why the petty officer had kept saying to me that I might want to take a shower. I could feel each day I had spent at sea shedding off my skin, layer by layer. My hair was completely dreadlocked, and there wasn't a thing I could do to untangle it. I still had a scab on my leg from the deep cut, but the wound on my head was almost healed. All the other wounds had healed—all but the wound to my heart. My body was lean, bony, skinny. Too skinny for me.

At the sink I brushed my teeth over and over; the cigars had stained them. I stared at the dark circles under my eyes and the angry-looking scar on my forehead as I brushed my teeth. Slowly even my teeth brightened to their natural white.

As I went back into the office I could see from the men's eyes that they were looking at a female—a female survivor, not a ravaged victim anymore.

After the written report was complete, Petty Officer Rodenhurst told me he was a newlywed and that he and his wife and daughter had an extra room in their house if I'd like to spend the night there, and to please call him Chris.

"Thank you, I'd—yes." I don't think I could have spent another night on *Hazana* now that I was clean and on land.

TWENTY

On Solid Ground

Chris's wife, Perry Rodenhurst, came to the station with her six-year-old daughter, Shannon, to pick me up. Perry was in her mid-twenties, attractive and lean, with blond shoulder-length hair. She was very gentle with me.

Perry showed me to the den of their modest home, where she tugged at the seat in the couch, unfolding it into a bed. She told me to make myself at home and pointed out the telephone. As Perry closed the door, she said to take my time with my calls.

I sat down on the edge of the bed and looked around the cozy room: a desk, framed family photographs, and books. How staid and normal it all seemed. Taking a deep breath I picked up the phone and dialed the operator to call my mother collect. It was two hours later there, early evening in California. Her number was busy. I tried my dad. No answer. I tried my mom again—still busy.

I was starting to lose it. Couldn't my mom feel my need to talk to her? It never dawned on me to ask the operator to make an emergency break through to my mother's number.

My grandparents had to be home, but what if they weren't? I wouldn't be able to stand it. I had to talk to someone—now.

My grandfather answered on the fourth ring. "Yellow."

"Grandpa, it's me. How are you?"

"How is *me*? How is *you*?"

"Oh, Grandpa, I'm not so good," I started bawling, "Richard is dead." Thus, my highly emotional phone call began.

Eventually my grandmother got on the line. I had to keep repeating myself because grief muffled my words. My mind was tired, confused, and still scared. Now what? Now what? pounded inside my brain. I'm sure I sounded crazy; I felt crazy. I wished I could crawl through the phone line and curl up in my granddad's lap.

After talking with my grandparents, I tried my mom again. Her number was still busy. I decided to call Richard's sister, Susie, in England, regardless of the hour. Jurrick, her husband, answered and told me she was out of town. He said he was relieved to hear my voice, for they had been worried. I collapsed in sobs at first, then sadly managed to give him the news in fairly accurate order. With both of us distraught and crying, Jurrick told me he had known Richard since he was a boy, that they were more than brothers-in-law. He was very upset, but volunteered to phone Richard's parents and let them know. I assured him I would call again later.

I decided to call *Hazana*'s owners, the Cromptons, that instant and get it over with. My hand shook violently as I tried to dial the number. Peter answered the phone. "Peter? A terrible thing has happened," I babbled. "Oh, this is Tami. You know, Tami . . . We got caught in the hurricane. Richard went overboard. He's gone." I barely took a breath between sentences. "*Hazana*'s masts are gone, she's a wreck. But she's floating."

"Oh dear, oh dear, oh no," Peter kept saying.

I had told the story so many times by now that my voice was almost flat, losing emotion, relying on logic. "*Hazana* will probably be considered totaled. You should contact your insurance company. Excuse me? Oh, I'm in Hilo. Hilo, Hawaii."

I could hear the devastation in Peter's voice as he told me how sorry he was to hear about Richard, that they had liked him so much. It was considerate of Peter not to question me about *Hazana*'s condition. All he said was that he and Christine would come immediately to Hawaii.

I finally got through to my mother. Her voice on the end of the line sent me into a tailspin. I could barely say "Mom . . ."

"Tami? My God, where have you been?" Her familiar chastise was a blessing. "I have been worried sick about you. I've gone to the Coast Guard station twice—where are you?"

"Oh Mom . . ."

"Honey? What is it? Are you okay?"

"Mom . . ." I must have wailed for ten minutes before her soothing, knowing voice could get me under control. She assured me over and over that Richard's death and the destruction of *Hazana* weren't my fault. I needed to hear that.

Finally, I was speechless. My mom insisted I give her the Rodenhursts' phone number. She was going to call the airport to book a flight immediately, and then she'd call me back. Her voice saying, "I love you, honey," echoed over and over as I lay down on the bed and waited for her to call back.

Shortly thereafter, she did; she'd be arriving in eleven hours. Would I be okay? Did I need anything? She wanted to talk to Perry. I said, "No. Just talk to me." So we talked on and on, until finally she said I should get some rest.

I lay down and stared at the white ceiling. Soon its flat surface became the sea rolling softly to the corners of the room, sailing down the decorated walls. My body, though stationary, rocked back and forth, back and forth. A light rapping on the door startled me. When I turned to look, Perry had opened it and was peeking in. I hadn't slept. I wanted to, but my mind wouldn't relax. She invited me to join them for dinner.

At the table, Shannon had obviously been told not to ask me any questions, but I could tell she was full of them by the way she stared at me and stroked her hair.

After a light meal, we all gathered around the television to watch the movie *Airplane*. As I sat in a comfortable beanbag chair, my mind kept wondering how one minute I could be stranded at sea and the next be in front of a television, watching a slapstick catastrophe movie. Somehow it all didn't make sense.

I couldn't make it through the movie, so I excused myself and went to bed, but I still couldn't sleep. I decided to try to reach my dad again. He answered, accepting the reverse charges.

"Dad?"

"Tami! Honey. Great timing—we just got in."

"Dad . . ."

"Hon, what's wrong? Are you okay? Where are you? We've been waiting to hear from you."

"Dad . . ." I burst out crying. "Richard's gone."

"What do you mean, Richard's gone?"

"Gone! The boat's trashed, and Richard's tether broke and he was swept overboard."

"Oh, my God!"

"That's what Richard said, and then the boat capsized. When I came to, he was gone."

"Oh, honey, where are you?"

"Hilo, Hawaii. I just got here today."

"I'll come right over. I can get there. . . ."

"No, it's okay, Mom's on her way." We talked for about an hour. Having to relive everything over and over was grueling, but healing too.

After we hung up, I was spent. I caught a glimpse of myself in the dresser mirror and tried to comb my fingers through my hair, but there was no way to put a dent in the matted mess. I gave up. All night long I tossed and turned, falling in and out of sleep. I wanted Richard, and I wanted the sun to come up. I wanted my mom to get there and take me home, take me away from all this and all that would inevitably still come. I wanted to get on with my life and have all this behind me—yet I knew there were things I had to do first. I could not escape.

Most of the night I stared at the pearlized reflections of the moon sweeping the wall and ceiling of the den. Somehow I felt more trapped being inside a house than I had felt outside, stranded on a boat.

———

The next morning I felt eager to return to *Hazana*. I missed her. Chris had already left for work. Perry, attempting to help me feel better about my appearance, gave me a dress to wear and helped me hide my hair under two stylishly tied scarfs. It felt odd to have a girlfriend again. She told me I looked better in the dress than she did, and even though I knew I looked odd, I appreciated the compliments—the confidence she was trying to instill in me.

We dropped Shannon off at school. Seeing all the children giggling, teasing each other and dashing about, brought tears to my eyes. I shook my head, for children have no clue what may unfold in their future and how hard life can be. Perry asked me if I was okay. I nodded yes and we took off for the Coast Guard station. When I went inside, Chris asked me if I'd seen all the reporters outside. "No," I said anxiously.

News channel, newspaper, and magazine reporters had lined the quay, waiting for me to show up. Chris escorted me out and stood by as I was interviewed. The reporters asked me to move here and there for the benefit of the cameras and videos. I was totally blown away by all the attention, and spent an hour and a half trying to accommodate the media: smiling, smiling, smiling as if everything were A-okay now. See how good I am, how cooperative. I had no idea my ordeal would cause such a stir.

After the reporters left, I escaped inside *Hazana*. There I let myself go and cried from deep down in my soul as I sat alone, looking at the shambles anew. What should I do? I didn't know what to do or where to go from here, or where to start.

Finally the time came for me to take a cab to the airport and meet my mother. Standing at the gate I was not surprised to see that my mom was the first passenger to disembark. She came rushing out and scooped me up in her arms. Hugging me, squishing me, crying all over me. She rocked me back and forth for the longest time and let me cry and cry while she cried with me. Many heads turned. They had no idea what a miracle this reunion was.

Brian, my mom's boyfriend, guided us out of the mainstream of foot traffic, and finally, as Mom and I calmed down, she introduced me to him. We hugged hello. There were tears of compassion in his blue eyes. Blue eyes—I had to look away.

We took a cab into town and checked into a nice hotel not too far from the quay. After lunch and a lot of talking and more crying, Mom decided we would deal with my dreadlocks first. The woman at the beauty salon in the hotel took one look as I pulled the scarves off my head and with a horrified expression said, "I can't do anything with that," then turned around and hurriedly disappeared into the back room. I stood there dumbfounded, and my mom said, "Come on honey, she's probably not any good anyway."

Outside the hotel, two reporters stopped us and introduced themselves. They asked if we had time for an interview and pictures. My mom said no, it was imperative we find a hair salon. They asked if they could tag along. "Sure, if you can keep up with us," my mom elbowed me with a chuckle.

We tried another beauty shop and they callously said they would have to shave my head. I burst into tears. I was not going to let anyone cut off all my hair; my identity was shattered as it was and I had already lost everything. There was no way I'd give up my hair. The reporters kindly did not document this but continued to follow us while we searched for another beauty salon. We came to a strip mall with a large sign posted out front that said, "GRAND OPENING—HOUSE OF LANTZ." We went inside and my mom firmly explained what had happened to me and how it could be to the salon's advantage to help us because of the interest the media had in my story. They agreed to try. As I was tilted back in the comfortable chair, my head was slathered with conditioner and detangler. I sat for four hours holding my scalp as three beauticians combed out the snarls as gently as they could. It hurt like hell. They stopped for the day when I could take no more. The next day I went back, and they worked on the opposite side. My scalp ached from all the tugging, but I wouldn't let them stop. After another four hours my hair hung long and straight. My mom held my cheeks, looked

Three beauticians worked for two days detangling my hair

deeply into my eyes, and said, "There's my beautiful baby girl." Finally, I started to feel like me. I couldn't thank House of Lantz enough, and they received great exposure on the cover of the local newspaper.

The Cromptons arrived the next day. I nervously paced the airport's waiting area. They hugged me hello when they disembarked, and I started weeping. We went directly to *Hazana.*

As we walked up to *Hazana,* all I could hear was Christine saying, "Oh, no. Oh, no." Peter was very quiet. Even with *Hazana* directly in front of their eyes, they still couldn't believe the damage.

"It's amazing she didn't sink," Peter said, looking back at me and marveling at the fact that it was a miracle I survived.

We sat in the cockpit and I told the whole story again. I tried to answer all their questions. Some explanations I could state clearly; others cracked the foundation and a flood of tears escaped. Peter had his camera and took a lot of pictures of *Hazana*. Christine appeared most overwrought. I had no control over my emotions and simply sat there, an endless stream of tears rolling down my face.

My mother came to *Hazana,* and I introduced her to the Cromptons. Seeing how upset I was and emotionally drained, she became "Mama Bear," insisting I come back to the hotel and rest. I went back to the hotel with her, leaving *Hazana's* owners to digest the tragedy and vent their own emotions.

The Cromptons arranged to have the items that survived shipped to England. They offered to deliver Richard's belongings to his family, if I wanted—whatever I cared to send along. I had taken most of my things off *Hazana* by then, but packing Richard's belongings once again took me on a psychological roller-coaster. I kept trying not to recall when he had worn a certain shirt or shorts. I would catch myself thinking what's the point of packing them up? But, I couldn't just leave everything, for these things might mean something to someone in his family.

The police were called in because the two of us had checked out of Tahiti, but only I had checked into Hawaii. As Richard was a British citizen missing in international waters, it was the job of police to investigate. They were kind as they questioned me intensively, but something was wrong: My timeline and theirs for the collision between Hurricane Raymond and *Hazana,* and for the events that happened afterward, did not mesh. Through diligent replay and replotting, they finally surmised that I must have been knocked out for twenty-seven hours, not the three hours I had always thought. That information shook me up all over again. Twenty-seven hours! No wonder the sea and weather were so much calmer when I came to. Where had my mind been, and my lover during that lost time? There was no way I could have saved Richard. I had been knocked out for more than a day. That meant I was one day off on my navigation, and still—by what, the grace of God, The Voice, myself—I had made it to Hawaii? The Voice was right, here was proof again that I was meant to live. But why hadn't The Voice told me I was knocked out for twenty-seven hours? Where was The Voice anyway?

A spokesman from *Hokusei Maru,* the Japanese research vessel that had towed me in, came knocking on *Hazana*'s hull as my mom and I were packing the last of Richard's possessions. The man, handing me a printed invitation for a reception that evening aboard the ship, apologized for the lateness, but it had taken him a while to find me.

Late that afternoon, Mom, Brian, and I arrived at the large commercial quay where the *Hokusei Maru* was docked. As we walked up to the ship we saw a table where guests—the men in dress whites, the women in gowns—were being greeted. We looked down uncertainly at our casual clothes as an Asian woman dressed in all her finery asked if she could help us. I handed her the invitation and said, "My name is Tami. . . ."

"Oh Tami, Tami!" She excitedly handed us name tags.

"I'm sorry we didn't dress better, we . . ."

"No matter. You fine, look fine. Please, come in." A man ushered us up the gangplank. On deck a magnificent array of food-adorned tables lined the perimeter of the aft deck, and a stage with a podium and microphone had been set up. Music played and people were dancing.

As we were escorted to an open bar, we received many inquisitive looks. I heard my name being repeated a couple of times, and then officers and mates from the ship started approaching me. I realized then that they hadn't recognized me as the ravaged woman they had rescued only a few days ago. Many people came up to see how I was doing and to meet my mother and Brian. I enjoyed a fancy Hawaiian cocktail with an umbrella and a red cherry. Ah, a whole red cherry. My mind flashed back to my pile of red cherry pieces from the can of fruit cocktail I opened after I dove under *Hazana* to check her hull, what, only a couple of weeks ago? Time was speeding by now, when it had passed so slowly back then. Mom and Brian danced while I shook what seemed like every hand on the ship.

The music suddenly ceased, and the first mate, tapping on the microphone, drew everyone's attention. He thanked the crowd for coming. Speaking in both English and Japanese, he told the audience they were celebrating the end of a successful joint research venture involving Japanese and Hawaiian college students. He went on to explain that what made this trip most miraculous was seeing a flare at dawn and coming upon a mastless sailboat and sailor, and coming to her—yes, *her*—aid. The crowd burst into applause and many people looked at me with wide smiles. I looked down and peripherally scanned the area—which way should I run?

My mom grabbed my arm. "Smile, honey. It's okay."

The captain walked up to the mike, and the mate translated for us as the captain spoke in animated Japanese. It was the first time in his career, the captain related, that he had seen and helped a shipwrecked sailor. It was an honor to be able to offer the service of his ship and crew, he said, and he would like to present me with a gift. I had no idea I would be honored at this reception. My mom gave me a little shove. I tried to hold my chin up as I walked onto the stage. The captain bowed. I bowed. He bowed. I bowed again. The audience chuckled, then the captain, then me. Gently the captain latched a necklace with a precious pearl pendant around my neck. Tears—the endless tears—flowed to the valley of my neck as I kissed his cheek in thanks. "Mauruuru," I said, for I didn't know how to say thank you in Japanese. Then with much cheer he proposed a banzai toast, wishing me ten thousand years of good luck.

I waffled among a rainbow of emotions. Here, I was being praised for surviving, but did anyone really understand that some days out there I hadn't wanted to live? Could anyone, besides my mother, see what great grief and guilt I shouldered over Richard's fate? I knew I was going to have to find a way to accept that it was okay that I had lived, but did I deserve ten thousand years of good luck?

I would have liked to say more, to the captain and crew, to expound on how I felt when I saw their ship and the crew's encouraging faces. But all I had the strength to do was finger the pendant and thank them for helping me. The cacophony of the applause was almost as nerve-wracking to me as the hurricane's roar had been, and when the mate approached and offered to take us on a tour of the ship, I eagerly accepted.

I took deep breaths as we climbed up to the pilothouse. Glancing around, I was in awe of how high we stood above the sea. I looked down and imagined how tiny and forlorn *Hazana* and I must have looked to the crew and students on the ship.

Tossing and turning that last night in Hilo, I was grateful to see the first hint of dawn. I crawled out of bed and put on the dress Richard had given me the night he proposed in Tahiti. Scrutinizing all the vases of beautiful flowers family and friends had sent me, I focused on one extraordinary bloom: a crimson rose. It wasn't a young, closed bud, but a mature blossom with petals gloriously reaching out to me. A single red rose, the international symbol of love. Its scent awoke fond memories, a bittersweet reminder that life goes on. I leaned over the blossom, its scent swirling in my senses like a warmed brandy on a chilly night. This was the rose for Richard.

I quietly slipped out of the hotel room. As I walked along the road, I felt anxious. If the mist left the air and the palette of the sunrise folded into daylight, the ambiance I needed would be lost. It became a race with the sun. I ran.

Winded, I arrived at the water's edge. I glanced at the horizon—the sun was surfacing as smoothly as a seal. I watched the swells lap against the breakwater, sending ocean spray over the rocks at its end, launching birds into flight. I inhaled the spicy perfume of the rose once again, and then started walking out on the jetty. I became acutely aware of how much I missed this time of day. More mornings than not, I had been awake on *Hazana,* steering or crying or meditating on the bow. It had been part of my salvation. I missed it. How could I leave this and go home without Richard? How am I going to live without him? My life was a mess. But I had survived. I *did* survive.

Coming to a spot that beckoned me, I crawled down a couple of boulders to a flat rock, hiked up my dress, and sat cross-legged a few feet above the sea. I followed the contours of the granite rocks as they slipped into the lavender water. The sea looked so calm. Richard's soul must love the freedom to wander all over it, all over the world. A glimmer of rouge highlighted a cheek of the sea. Was that Richard smiling at me? Oh, Richard, if only . . . If only my soul had been meant to soar the heaven, earth, and sea with you, I'd be there. You know that, don't you? For forty-one days on the ocean I tried to understand what happened to you—to us. The only thing I could figure out is we fell in love. It's as simple as that. Nothing happened to us but falling madly, passionately in love. I want to say to you I will never, ever, love again, but I am weak. I'm weak, Richard. I don't want to be alone. I don't like being alone. No one to share a sunrise with, a dance with . . . I want to be a mother one day, then a grandmother. I want to watch my garden grow and pet baby puppies and old cats and sing Christmas carols with friends. I want to love life as much as I loved it with you—if that's possible. I have to let go—I have to let you go.

I watched the sun kiss the horizon one last time before it sprang into the air and I sprang to my feet. Pulling off the twine ring Richard had given me, I pressed it to my lips. "I swear to God I will always love you, Richard." Choking on my tears I slid the ring up the stem of the perfect rose. Gently I drew the leaves back through the ring—the circle of love—making sure the stems of the leaves held the ring in place. I inhaled its fragrance one last time and then tossed the rose out into the sea. I watched it drift away from me, bobbing on the textured ocean. The rose and the ring had a mission—to find Richard. The shrill cries of gulls brought me back. I watched them soar and dive, checking out my offering, before I admitted to myself that I, too, had a mission. It was time to go home.

TWENTY-ONE

Home at Last

I never really said good-bye to *Hazana*. The word *Hazana* means "deed, exploit, or feat" in Spanish, and in hindsight she had, uncannily, been named appropriately. If *Hazana* had not been built with such structural integrity she would have sunk and I would have gone down with her. I cannot express in words my respect and love for *Hazana* and my admiration for Anne Wever and the shipwrights who built her in Wever's shipyard in the Netherlands.

It was a whirlwind exit. The next thing I knew I was on a plane headed for the mainland. I didn't look out the window, down at the sea I had crawled across trying to reach land. I slept, curled up under a blanket, on two seats across from my mom and Brian, keeping my anxiety close to me.

At the San Diego airport, I stepped off the plane to see the tarmac crowded with people, lights, and cameras. My dad rushed up, tears on his face, and grabbed me and hugged me and hugged me and hugged me. He then guided me to my grandparents, who, as always, knew the right things to say. Many of my family and friends were there to greet me, congratulate me for making it—surviving. I can't remember a great deal from this reunion except an overwhelming feeling of love and support. It was much like The Voice promised me it would be. I spent that night at my grandparents' house in my old bedroom, and then the next day went home to Mom's.

Over the next couple months, as I struggled to rebuild my life, I found I had no life. I was floundering, running around like a madwoman, trying to escape pain and indecision. I stayed home for Thanksgiving and Christmas, all the while feeling an overpowering compulsion to go to Richard's family and explain to them face to face what had happened; it was the least I could do. So, in early January I flew to England.

I landed in London and caught a train to Southampton, where *Hazana*'s owners, Peter and Christine Crompton, lived. In my train window, England's groomed landscape— so different from the lush wildness of the South Pacific— rushed by.

The Cromptons' home was impressive. They were gracious hosts, doing everything to make me comfortable. Peter asked if I'd like to go with them and some friends on a sailboat race around the Isle of Wight. The last boat I had been on was *Hazana*. The Cromptons' insurance company had sold *Hazana* in Hawaii. They now had a thirty-six-foot sloop

Arriving at home

that they used for local races and weekend cruising. I slept on the decision, but strangely enough, I missed the omnipresence of the sea, so I agreed to go. We didn't win the race, but we didn't come in last either. We had a fine time, although the motion of the boat jolted latent memories of briskly sailing with Richard. I forced myself to stay in the moment and not to regress. None of the Cromptons' friends mentioned *Hazana* or the capsize to me, although I'm sure they all knew about it.

I didn't stay with the Cromptons long, as I was anxious to get to Cornwall and Richard's family. The Cromptons could tell I was still suffering; they were compassionate people.

From Southampton I took the train to Cornwall. I stayed

at Richard's sister Susie's house. It was a tearful time. Susie and Richard had been so close—it was hard for her to believe he was dead. She could see I was emotionally brittle—smiling one minute, tearful the next—so we walked and talked, and shared stories.

Richard's father, Mr. Sharp, came over to Susie's shortly after I arrived. As he walked through the dining room door into the living room I stood up, not knowing what to do. Should I hug him or shake his hand? I looked for a resemblance to Richard, but I didn't see one. I started crying and then surprised myself by saying, "How about a hug." He hugged me and patted my back. After a minute, Susie helped ease the situation by having us sit down at the table for lunch. As we ate, the conversation remained light; no one mentioned Richard. All I wanted to do was talk about Richard and have them ask me about him, but it was as if a stone wall of denial had been put before me, so I held in my tongue.

The next night we met for dinner at the Sharps'. Their home was impressive too. The meal was well thought out and delicious, but I nervously picked at my food. My stomach knotted in anticipation of what I would say to the gathered family.

After dinner we all sat in the living room, and I finally described the terrible incident, blow by blow. I explained how we tried to outrun the hurricane and what a hero Richard had been as he fought so bravely to keep *Hazana* and me from any harm. The family sat and listened. Not a single question was asked. Perhaps their silence was acceptance of the tragedy—I don't know. I was there because in my heart I felt I owed this trip to Richard. He would have wanted me to tell his family firsthand how bravely he died. I know their pain was as deep as mine. I know it could not have been deeper—different yes, but not deeper. I wanted so desperately to connect with them, to find a piece of Richard that was still alive. It was hard to face the fact that an extension of Richard did not exist, which only confirmed to me how unique he really was.

A couple of nights later I went with the Sharp family to dinner at the home of friends of theirs who had known Richard since he was a boy. The woman took me aside and with tears in her eyes told me how much she had loved him. She said she and her husband had been proud of Richard for taking off and living his dream. She too could only shake her head in dismay at his sad and untimely death. It meant a great deal to me that she felt comfortable enough to share her feelings with me.

I met with the Sharps' family lawyer and he explained to me that Richard had left *Mayaluga* to Jurrick, Susie's husband, in his will. Later that night I told Jurrick that if he wanted to sell *Mayaluga* I would buy her, because I wanted to continue to sail her around the world, as Richard and I had planned to do. Jurrick told me that we'd work it out.

Richard's father never cried in front of me, nor did Richard's stepmother. Close to two months had passed since they learned of Richard's death; perhaps I was taking them backward in their healing process and not forward. I finally realized that I couldn't help them with their healing and they couldn't help me with mine.

When I returned to San Diego, two weeks later, there was a message for me from Peter and Ann Deeth, whom Richard and I had met in Tahiti. I called them back in Antigua, the West Indies, where they owned a hotel. They had seen my interview with Diane Sawyer on the CBS News and they expressed their heartfelt condolences over the loss of Richard. They asked if I planned on going back to Tahiti. I said yes, and that I'd still like to do the brightwork on their boat, *Petrana,* as I had agreed to before Richard and I left Tahiti, if they still wanted it done. They did.

This conversation set me in motion. My parents accepted the fact that I needed to go back to Tahiti, where all my worldly possessions were, but, more important, where our *Mayaluga* was—waiting for me.

Flying into Papeete was emotional for me. As I stared down into the sparkling aqua sea, I could recall every precious moment I had spent with Richard. I grabbed my carry-on bag from the overhead bin, hurried off the plane and out of the airport, and hailed a taxi. I could not get to *Mayaluga* quickly enough. The cab took me to Mataiea. No one was home at Antoinette and Haipade's when I got there, so I walked down to the beach and stood. There floated *Mayaluga,* the beautiful sloop Richard had built from bow to stern. Tears rolled down my face. Tossing my bag in our old dinghy, I dragged it down to the water and rowed like crazy to get to her.

As I opened the companionway hatch, warm air, like a sigh of relief, escaped, brushing past my face. I took a couple of steps down the ladder, sat down, and sobbed every last tear out of me. How could Richard not be here? Had I really thought he'd miraculously show up? I felt so totally alone once again.

A couple of hours passed. As I sat in the cockpit I heard the Topa family arrive home. I watched them for a while, and then felt a yearning to go say hello. As I rowed to shore, they all ran out to greet me. It was both a happy and a sad reunion. They had heard about Richard's death. I thanked them for taking such good care of *Mayaluga* and explained I was back now to complete Richard's and my voyage around the world. They did not like the idea of my staying out on the boat alone, at least not while she was moored so near their house. Antoinette convinced me to stay on shore for a while and live with their family. She was right, it was better for me to be part of a family unit.

Every morning started like a train: The wheels would slowly begin to chug until the whole household was up to full speed. Crammed into the car were those going to work and those going to school. We'd first head into town and go to Haipade's favorite spot for *poisson cru*—marinated fish—and croissants for breakfast. Then they would drop me off at the boatyard where I was refinishing the brightwork on *Petrana*.

The *Petrana* was a forty-eight-foot Cheoy Lee ketch.

I stripped, bleached, and sanded with great care and then applied ten coats of varnish. I was so focused on the project that I didn't realize the effect of the blazing tropical sun and I fainted from heat stroke. A man working on another boat saw me collapse and took me to the medical center, where the staff had me drink water and lie down with a cool cloth on my head. The second time I started feeling faint, I realized what was happening and quit work for the day. I wasn't as strong as I used to be.

Refinishing *Petrana* was the best thing for me at that time. It kept me functioning and away from wallowing in depression when everywhere I turned I was reminded of Richard. When the Deeths arrived they were thrilled at how great *Petrana* looked. They launched her right away, and we spent many nights sitting in the cockpit talking. It felt good to reminisce with people who knew Richard and had shared good times with us.

During this time I wrote letters to Jurrick, Richard's brother-in-law, trying to reach some agreement about purchasing *Mayaluga*. Sadly, Jurrick and I could never agree on a price. He said he couldn't afford to give her away. Meanwhile I was adamantly advised by people who had my well-being at heart not to pay a fortune for her, no matter what sentimental value was involved. It was a sad, confusing, and frustrating time.

Jurrick wrote to tell me he was hiring a man who had previously completed a circumnavigation to fly to Tahiti and sail *Mayaluga* back to England for him. I can't describe how forlorn I felt. I was given a certain amount of time to get my possessions off the boat. I felt kicked off *Mayaluga*—our *Mayaluga*. I could feel Richard's soul crying.

As I was boatless and with no direction, the Deeths invited me to meet them in Bora Bora and crew to Fiji with them. I jumped at the offer. I took what was mine off *Mayaluga* and stored it at the Topas' while I decided what to sell and what to ship home. I shipped home my beautiful shell collections, tapas we had purchased in the Marquesas, pictures, letters, and items I couldn't part with. With the last of my possessions loaded in the dinghy I went below in *Mayaluga* and knelt at the V-berth. I draped my arm along the cushion and rested my cheek on the bed. This was where I learned about real love. Oh Richard—Richard, Richard, Richard.

With a heavy heart I climbed on a plane and never looked back as I took off for Bora Bora.

The Deeths sailed *Petrana* from Tahiti to Bora Bora with some of their family on board. After their family left and I flew in, we sailed *Petrana* for the atoll of Mopelia, which is also part of the Society Islands group.

Mopelia was magical. We swam in the clear sparkling lagoon and walked the white sand beaches. I was beginning to heal. We collected eggs from the thousands of tern eggs lying on the coral reefs. The eggs are delicious to eat, once you get over the very orange color they turn when they are cooked.

While I spent hours shelling in the sand I contemplated a

lot. Mostly my thoughts flowed to Richard and the precious time we shared doing what I was now doing alone. I still felt so empty and confused, but I knew that I was following the right path by getting back to the sea and to the lifestyle I loved.

From Mopelia we sailed for the atoll Suwarrow to see the home of the famous hermit, the late Tom Neale. When we arrived we found the yacht *Fleur d'ecosse* moored in the bay. She belonged to Anne and Ron Falconer, whom Richard and I had met while cruising the Marquesas.

Walking up the beach, we followed crushed coral paths to Neale's hut, where we came upon a large slab of stone. The inscription on the stone read: 1959–1977 TOM NEALE LIVED HIS DREAM ON THIS ISLAND.

Anne and Ronald had set up house in the two-room hut—Anne was about ready to deliver their first baby so they were afraid to move on. There were chickens running around, and Tom Neale's small garden flourished with vegetables and tropical plants. The Falconers were happy to see me again and to meet the Deeths. Inside the hut they showed us the logbook that passing sailors signed as evidence they had visited the atoll. It was fascinating to see how many sailors had come from far and wide to explore Suwarrow. Even survivors of yachts gone aground on the reefs had lived in the hut until rescued.

We stayed at Suwarrow for about three days and then sailed for American Samoa, where we could reprovision on our way to Fiji. The harbor at Pago Pago was dirty and lined with tuna factories, but on an all-day hike over the saddle of the mountain to the other side of the island, we found gorgeous white-sand beaches.

With food lockers bulging, we headed for the Vava'u Islands in the Kingdom of Tonga, where we rendezvoused with the Deeths' son, the young skipper of a privately owned hundred-foot yacht, the *Catalina*. The yacht had six crew members and all the toys one could ever wish to play with: Lazer sailboats, windsurfers, and fast Cigarette boats, to name just a few. We enjoyed picnics on the beach, eating gourmet food, and playing with all the toys.

Sadly, the Deeths' vacationing time was coming to an end. When I called my mother and learned that she and Brian were going to get married, I decided to go home. I was pleased she wanted me to be her maid of honor. The Deeths found a safe anchorage and a caretaker for *Petrana*. When they left I stayed on to paint the boat's interior as I had agreed to do. Then I went home to San Diego for the wedding.

On the flight home I wondered if I would ever get used to being in a remote area one minute and flying into suburbia the next. How many miles had I crossed over the past six months? All I ever had wanted was to sail forever with Richard.

It was wonderful to see my mother in love. She and Brian were married at Brian's parents' house overlooking the Pacific Ocean on Sunset Cliffs, Point Loma, California. I wore a burgundy wraparound silk skirt with hand-painted birds of paradise. The painted flowers flowed around my hips and up onto a matching blouse. My mother wore an ivory lace dress that showed off her shapely figure. She looked beautiful—I was so proud and happy for her.

Brian, now my stepfather, had enrolled in navigation school in San Diego, to get his hundred-ton captain's license. My mom suggested I enroll too. Why not? I had moved onto a friend's yacht to give the newlyweds some space, and I wasn't sure what I wanted to do next. I was twenty-four years old.

I ended up talking to an old friend from the *Sofia* days, Evan, who was skippering a 106-foot three-masted schooner, *Rambler*, on the East Coast. The company he worked for, Ocean Research and Education Society (ORES), was looking for licensed mates, and Evan said that if I got my hundred-ton license they would probably hire me. So, I enrolled.

I was the only woman in the class of about fifteen men. I went to school three nights a week, three hours a night, for eight weeks. I found it difficult to study. I couldn't seem to concentrate. So Brian helped by studying with me.

We both passed the captain's exam and three weeks later I was second mate aboard the research vessel *Rambler*. She was doing scientific work on Silver Bank, an ocean reef about 200 miles northeast of the Dominican Republic.

I felt relieved to finally have some direction. I was aboard *Rambler* for three months, from the Dominican Republic to Gloucester, Massachusetts, her home port.

I signed on *Rambler* for another six months as first mate, and we sailed from Gloucester, Massachusetts, up to a province of Canada, Labrador, and back. Sailing around icebergs was exciting; somehow, the adventure helped thaw my frozen heart. After that six months it was time to move on.

⸺

Back in San Diego, I spent the next year working with my mother and Brian in their yacht management business and skippering a trimaran charter boat named *Continental I*. But after all my traveling and exploring I longed for a slower-paced, intimate setting. A location that had more fresh air and nature than concrete.

During that year, I took a trip to San Juan Island, in the northwest corner of the state of Washington, to visit my friend Laura. I was amazed that she never locked her front door and could take long walks in the forest without fear. She was constantly waving hello to other islanders, who always smiled and waved back. I saw deer, wild turkeys, eagles, otters, and whales. My heart sang; it felt like home. Here was the ocean I could never leave and God's green earth I longed to love all in one place.

Back in San Diego, the Pacific Northwest lingered in my mind and lulled me to sleep at night. I recalled how the island's dense emerald forest meandered down to the sea. It seemed to beckon to me.

A few months later I moved to San Juan Island, Washington. Now at last, I was really home.

I took long walks up Mount Young and along South Beach, or through the University of Washington lab property, always resting at some gorgeous vista of the sea. I rarely cried now, and would feel amazed when I'd catch myself grinning or smiling—caught up in a wonderful memory of my past with Richard.

Finally the day came when, near the water's edge, I saw a different reflection of myself. The ripply wind-wakes ruffled my mirrored image. "Look at you," I said aloud to myself, "you look good. It's about time. Time to take the lock off your heart now too. Let somebody else love you; love somebody else. It's okay. Richard wants you to."

I fell back like I had when the beady-eyed black tip sharks snuck up on me while shelling in Raroia.

Was that The Voice talking to me? Or was it me talking to me? All I know is, I felt as if a fever had broken, the sense of relief was indescribable. I jumped up and ran along the remote trail. When I came to a point of land with a view of insurmountable beauty, I froze. Then like an erupting volcano, I stretched my arms wide open to the sky, tilted my head back, and roared like an animal set free—forcing every last drop of sorrow from my soul.

TWENTY-TWO

Aftermath

Today, I am often asked to speak to yacht clubs. They want the "hurricane survivor" to tell her story in person. The first thing I stress when I give these talks is that I am not telling my story to scare any would-be blue-water sailors, but to encourage anyone who holds the dream of cruising to go. The cruising life is complete—full of adventure, education, freedom, and fun. I emphasize that I share my story to inform everyone who goes to sea, man or woman, of the importance of being prepared to assume the captain's role. It is everyone's responsibility on board a sailing vessel, including a woman's, to learn all they can about operating the vessel as well as navigation. It's crucial to learn the fundamentals of using a chart, interpreting GPS coordinates, and charting a line of position. In today's world of high-tech electronic equipment, having a sextant on board is a rarity. However, heading across the ocean is a huge undertaking, and being prepared is key. In the end, the items that saved my life didn't require batteries.

The question I'm most frequently asked when I speak is, "What would you do differently, if you had to do it all over again?"

My first instinct is to say I'd ask Richard to forget the delivery job and go on with our own plans. But that's only with hindsight. So I answer honestly that I would not tease Mother Nature by attempting a long blue-water sail during any portion of hurricane season. I stress that Mother Nature is bigger than any of us, and that it's important to cruise within the sailing seasons.

The second question I'm asked is, "If you were in the same situation again at sea (God forbid), what would you do differently? Turn around? Put out a drogue? Have both of you go below? What?"

I have to shake my head at that question because it's a hard one to answer. I don't have a straight answer. I wish Richard would have come below with me, but it's hard to relinquish control of the helm, especially when you feel the worst is about to be over and the situation is somewhat under control. We flat-out did the best we could. So I don't know what we could have done differently.

I will never understand why Richard died and I lived, except that he saved my life by having me go below. Though his life was cut short, he made such an impression on me, and he taught me to follow my heart by tossing off the dock lines of normal, everyday life and sailing away in search of adventure. Richard will always be my hero, and I will always love him. I am grateful to be alive, and in his memory I continue to follow his example, living my life today with passion, love of the sea, and a commitment to finding light even in my darkest hours.

Through my story, I hope that you too will find inspiration and strength. I believe it was fate—God's will—that I was spared. It was not my time. And after spending forty-one days alone, the only consistent message I had from God, or a higher power, or the universe, or The Voice, is that we, as individuals, *do* each have our own destiny. I believe that God does work "in mysterious ways." That is my belief—the tack I sail my life on.

Epilogue

These days, I live a happy and harmonious life in Friday Harbor, San Juan Island, Washington, where I own and operate two successful businesses. Being an entrepreneur gives me a sense of accomplishment, and I love working at my own pace, being my own boss, and having happy customers.

In 1992 I fell in love with a talented man, Ed Ashcraft, and we married in 1994. He asked me to dance at the Grange Hall one Friday night. His arm felt strong around my waist, his grip confident and secure. He looked me directly in the eyes and smiled so warmly I melted. He too has blue eyes, only they are not lapis lazuli, they're lighter, softer, clear blue like the sky on a cloudless sunny day. One dance led to another, and another. We moved so perfectly together, we flowed.

Ed builds dream homes for clients and has built one for

us. He treats me like a queen at the most astonishing times. He loves me deeply and we share similar dreams and goals. We are lovers and friends, and we make each other laugh.

But my greatest achievements, beyond surviving the hurricane, are having given birth to our daughters—Kelli, in 1995, and Brook, in 1997.

We all love being out on the water, and one of my fondest memories is sailing in our twenty-six-foot quarter-tonner, *Blondie,* Kelli sitting on my lap on the starboard side of the cockpit. We were on a beam reach when she eagerly reached out for the teak-and-spruce tiller. "You want to help me steer, Kelli?" I asked as I guided her tiny hand onto the smooth surface of the arc-shaped wood. Slowly drawing the tiller toward us, I said, "This is upwind."

"Upwind," she repeated.

Then, pushing the tiller away, I whispered with a sigh, "And this is downwind."

Kelli turned and looked up at me with her daddy's big, clear blue eyes, sensing something different in my voice, perhaps a wistfulness. I looked down into her beautiful, innocent face, wishing I could promise her that her life would always sail on an even keel, but I knew I had to tell her the truth. I kissed her satiny forehead and confessed, "Life is like sailing, love. It's upwind and downwind." She smiled and I smiled. Daddy eased the sheets then went below to get Brook, who had just woken from her nap.

Brook was born on a harvest moon at 12:45 P.M., with the amniotic sac still intact.

Smooth sailing

"It's a rarity," my midwife, Melinda, told us. "There's an old wives' tale, do you know it?"

"No," we replied.

"The old wives' tale is that a child born in the caul will never drown or be lost at sea."

My breath caught—Melinda didn't know about my tragedy at sea. I remember reaching for Brook, taking her in my arms and scrutinizing her newborn face. She was crinkled up, damp, crying—fair-haired like Ed, Kelli, and me. I put her to my breast and hugged her securely.

Thank God she will never be lost at sea. For like my mother had said to me, "Tami, if you'd been lost at sea, I would have never, ever, ever, stopped looking for you."

Glossary

AFT Near the rear or back of the boat.

AMIDSHIPS In the middle of the boat, where she is widest.

ANEMOMETER An instrument that measures wind velocity.

ATOLL A ring-shaped low-lying reef that encloses a lagoon.

BABYSTAY A stay running from the foredeck to the mast solely to support the mast.

BACKSTAY The wire giving aft, or rear, support to the mast.

BACKWINDED Wind flowing from a forward sail onto the lee side, or opposite side to which the wind is blowing, of an after sail.

BAROMETER An instrument that measures atmospheric pressure.

BEAM REACH To sail when the wind is hitting amidship, or the side of the boat.

BEAT To sail in the direction from which the wind is blowing, or as close to the wind as efficiently possible. Often making progress by sailing in a zigzag line.

BILGE The lowest inner part of a boat's hull.

BINNACLE A support or pedestal that houses the compass, usually located in the cockpit.

BLOCK A pulley.

BOOM A horizontal pole that extends the foot of a sail.

BOOM CRUTCH A support that holds the boom in place when it's not in use.

BOWSPRIT A spar extending forward from the bow of a ship.

BRIGHTWORK Boat woodwork that is sanded and varnished, not painted.

BULKHEAD A wall separating a boat's cabins that provides athwartships, or side to side, support to the hull.

CLEAT A wooden, metal, or plastic fitting to which lines are secured.

CLEVIS PIN A pin secured in a U-shaped fitting to hold an item of rigging.

CLEW The lower corner of a sail, where the sheets, or lines, attach.

COAMING A low wall around a cockpit, designed to keep out water.

COCKPIT The sunken area of a boat's deck where the wheel or tiller is located.

COME ABOUT To change the boat's direction by heading into the wind until the sails swing across the boat.

COMPANIONWAY The entry and steps from the deck to the inside of the boat.

CUTTER A sailing boat having one mast, with a mainsail and two headsails, a staysail, and a jib.

DEAD RECKONING (D.R.) Calculations of the course sailed, the distance run, the drift of the current, and the time spanned to determine a boat's position at sea.

DODGER A windshield, usually of canvas and clear plastic or fiberglass and Plexiglas, used to reduce wind and spray in the cockpit. (*Also see* windscreen.)

DOLDRUMS No wind.

D-RING Stainless steel D-shaped ring through which a rope may be passed.

DROGUE A drag device, such as a long rope with knots in it, trailed behind a boat to help slow the boat down.

EPIRB Emergency position-indicating radio beacon.

FERRO-CEMENT A mixture of cement, sand, and pozzolan, or fine aggregate, troweled onto a framework of rods, pipes, and chicken wire.

FOOT The lower edge of a sail.

FORE In front; opposite of aft.

FORESTAY A stay, usually a stainless steel cable, that runs from the bow, or forward part of a boat, to the top of the mast. (*Also see* stay.)

GALLEY Kitchen on a boat.

GENOA Genoa jib, also called genny. A large triangular headsail that extends well aft of the mast.

GOOSENECK The universal joint that holds the boom to the mast.

HALYARD A line used to hoist a sail and/or flag.

HAWSER A very thick rope.

HEAD (1) Bathroom. (2) The top corner or edge of a sail.

HEADSAIL A triangular sail set forward of the mainmast.

HEAVE-TO To lash the tiller one way and backwind the headsail the other way, putting you in a stationary position.

HEEL To lean, to list to one side, as in "heeling like a yacht in a gale."

HELM   The tiller or steering wheel of a boat.

HYDRAULICS   Machinery operated by the movement and force of liquid.

JACK LINE   A line or cable that runs the length of the boat; crew members can clip a safety-harness tether to the line for free range of movement on deck.

JIB   A triangular sail set on a stay forward of the mast.

KEEL   The fore-and-aft member along the center of the bottom of the boat, on which the structure of the boat is built.

KETCH   A two-masted boat with the mizzen mast stepped, or placed, forward of the rudderpost. (*Also see* mizzen mast.)

KNOT   A measurement of speed, 1 nautical mile per hour, about 1.15 statute miles per hour.

LEE   The side opposite to that from which the wind blows.

LINE   Nautical term for rope.

LIST   To lean to one side, as in "the boat was listing badly."

LOGBOOK (LOG)   The record book kept of a voyage.

LUFF   (1) The side of the sail attached to the mast. (2) The act of pointing the boat into the wind, spilling air out of the sails.

MIZZEN MAST   The mast closest to the stern on a ketch or yawl.

MONKEY FIST   The knot on the end of a rope, used for throwing.

NAV STATION The area inside the boat designated for navigational purposes.

PITCHPOLE To somersault in the sea, said of a boat.

PORT The left side of a boat.

PULPIT A stainless-steel guardrail around the bow or stern of the boat.

REEF To reduce the size of a sail to lessen the area exposed to the wind.

RODE Rope attached to the anchor chain.

RUDDER An underwater vertically hinged plate of metal or wood that is adjusted by the helm to steer the boat.

RUDDERPOST The vertical shaft of a rudder, allowing it to pivot when the tiller or steering gear is operated.

RUN OFF To turn downwind and sail with the wind on your back.

SAT-NAV Satellite navigation. An instrument that receives coordinates from satellites for navigation.

SCHOONER A fore-and-aft-rigged boat having two or more masts, with the mainmast being the tallest or equal to the foremast.

SEAT LOCKER Compartment for stowage located under a seat.

SET Pushed by the current.

SHACKLE A metal U-shaped fitting with an eye in each of its arms through which a pin can be screwed or driven.

SHAKEDOWN CRUISE A test sail.

SHEET A line used to control a sail's position.

SHROUD A wire rope secured from the side of a boat to the masthead, to provide athwartships, or side, support to the mast.

SLOOP A fore-and-aft-rigged boat with one mast and one forward sail or headsail.

SOLE The floor of a boat's cabin.

SPAR Any pole supporting the sail of a boat: for example, a mast, bowsprit, or boom.

SPINNAKER A three-cornered sail made of light, stretchy sailcloth, used when running downwind.

SPREADER A wood or metal strut on a mast that keeps the rigging stretched apart.

SQUALL A windstorm, usually brief and violent and often with rain.

STANCHION Metal poles attached to the deck to support the lifelines.

STARBOARD The right side of a boat.

STAY A wire rope that supports a mast forward and aft.

STAYSAIL A triangular sail used between the jib and the mainsail.

TABERNACLE The housing on deck that supports the heel and pivot of a mast so it can be lowered to the deck.

TACK (1) To alter course. (2) The lower-forward corner of a fore-and-aft sail.

TETHER A line attached from a safety vest to the boat.

THRU-HULL A fitting that runs from the interior to the exterior of the hull.

TILLER A lever used to steer a boat.

TOERAIL The raised edge around the deck of a boat.

TRADE WINDS An extremely consistent system of winds occupying most of the tropics.

TRIM To pull in or ease out the sheet of a sail so that the sail will set properly.

V-BERTH A berth in the bow of the boat.

VHF A very high frequency radio, effective, usually, for short distances and within line of sight.

WATERLINE A horizontal line on the hull of a boat, indicating the designed displacement.

WINDLASS A winch that has a horizontal drum and can handle chain cable.

WINDSCREEN A dodger that blocks the wind. (*Also see* dodger.)

Acknowledgments

Without the help and dedication of many people, the thought of putting my story into a book would have been left just that—a thought. Through all the twists and turns, this book has taken on a life of its own. I would like to thank the many people who have helped it unfold, and my friends and family for their never-ending support.

I am especially grateful to Marie Ashcraft for earnestly editing every revision. To Oscar Lind, who has been a beacon in the fog. Lynne Mercer, for her "walk your talk" challenge. Debbie Bledsoe, whose energy is contagious. Mitzi Johnson, for her conceptualization. Steve and Eric Brandt, who have given me invaluable guidance and inspiration. Teri Thompson, Cathy Johnson, Mary Stone, Neva Beach, and Gerard Woldtvedt for the hours of editing that kept this project on course. Bruce Conway, who is truly a magician with a Mac and whose advice was spot on. Dorothea Auguztiny, an inspirational force cheering me on.

A generous thank-you to my agent, Jill Grinberg, for her choice of vacation destinations, which changed my life. To Peternelle van Arsdale, for her gentle pen. What a gem to work with.

Thank you to Jon Cassir at CAA for taking this on and thinking out of the box. Thanks to Jessica Sindler and the team at Dey Street Books for their patience and direction, and to Tom Killingbeck and the team at HarperCollins UK for their support.

Much aloha to Aaron Kandell and Jordan Kandell, whose steadfast friendship and persistence is how the movie version of *Adrift* became a reality. Thank you to Baltasar Kormákur, whose creative passion and attention to detail make him one of the best.

My appreciation and awe to the cast of *Adrift*, including Shailene Woodley and Sam Claflin, who worked tirelessly out on the open, unforgiving ocean day after day. Thanks to the crew and to the behind-the-scenes community, who were there at a moment's notice for support, and truly vital to the production's success. I am forever grateful to STX Productions, who stepped up and made my dream a reality.

I am truly indebted to Susea McGearhart for her enthusiasm and focus on this project, without whom this book would still be just a dream. Thank you to Gene Gearhart, for casting Susea off on this long writing voyage.

Thank you to my family. To my mother for giving me

drive and the strength to tackle life head-on. To my grandma and grandpa Oldham for instilling their values and being the stability in my life. To my father, living proof of how to have fun in life, and for his moral support. To my little brother, Dane (who is not so little), who gave me the will to live when I was at my lowest.

To the love of my life, Ed: Thank you for your total commitment to me and our family. Your patience through this project was staggering.

Thanks to my girls, Kelli and Brook, who have taught me about unconditional love and who turned out to be the real reason I survived.